The Splendor
That Was Africa

THE
SPLENDOR THAT
WAS AFRICA

by
Ricky Rosenthal

1967
Oceana Publications, Inc.
Dobbs Ferry, New York

Acknowledgements

To Mrs. Margaret Bender whose encouragement and insight guided my own quest and to Mia Aurbakken, a dear friend. To Ambassador and Mrs. Eamonn L. Kennedy, exceptional friends, upon whose intelligence, patience, and energy I drew upon so heavily on my trip to West Africa. To Ted Morello, my colleague, with thanks for his thoughtful assistance, and to Kwame Adeusi-Poku whose help, and special perspective were invaluable to me. To those at the University of London (School of Oriental and African Studies), The American Museum of Natural History, The American Geographical Society, the Schomburg Collection of the New York Public Library, The Jewish Theological Seminary Library and those who assisted me at the Dag Hammarskjold Library, and to the director of the Map Collection in particular. To my husband for his help with translations, and especially for his forbearance. To those African statesmen who found time for discussion with me when they had none to spare, while participating in the work of the United Nations, I am deeply indebted, and to the many African friends at the United Nations whose own enthusiasm and enlightened outlook reinforced my own interest.

A NOTE ON THE ARTIST

Solomon Irein Wangboje was born in Avbiosi, Iuleha, near Benin in Nigeria. At present he is completing a doctorate in the field of art education at New York University.

After receiving his diploma in Fine Arts from the College of Technology in Zaria (Northern Nigeria) he subsequently worked as a Publications Artist for the Nigerian government, and at another time served as Design and Art Supervisor for the Nigerian Television Service. His first visit to the United States was in response to a Cranbrook Academy of Art scholarship in 1961. In 1963 he returned home and completed his Master's degree in Fine Arts. He has had several exhibitions in the United States. He works in oils as well as in Lino and woodcut.

The motif of the cover, says Mr. Wangboje, is seen through the silhouette of the camel to enhance and emphasize that we are viewing our subject matter from a distance in historical time. The camel, a symbol of desert transportation, was also of great value. The buildings in the background depict traditional architecture of the area described in the book. In the foreground is a man seated on a camel, holding a sword with his luggage packed about him, this was, and still is, a common sight. In the lower half of the foreground, on both sides are two symbols derived from the design on Ashanti goldweights, between these symbols is a passing pictorial reference to the many crafts practiced in the area.

Contents

Preface

Teachers of African studies will welcome Ricky Rosenthal's *THE SPLENDOR THAT WAS AFRICA,* which is one of the first few pioneering works in this country dealing with a neglected area of knowledge concerning a continent about which both the general public and the schools are clamoring for less fictional and more factual information.

The book deals with the pre-colonial West African Empires of Ghana, Mali and Songhai, which flourished during the European "Dark Ages". These have been treated, of course, by Professor Elliot Skinner in his *A GLORIOUS AGE IN AFRICA,* (1965) published by Zenith Books; but the two authors address themselves to different audiences. Professor Skinner's book was, it seems to me, written primarily with young school children in mind. Mrs. Rosenthal's book, on the other hand, is aimed more at the adult scholar.

She begins the book, properly, as one must in such an undertaking, by asking the reader to "strip away the myth that Africa south of the Sahara had no history before the coming of the Europeans in the 14th century . . . and to . . . tear up the roadway of African history that has been paved with the notion that whatever history Africa did have was neither intelligible nor significant." Indeed, her task of debunking begins when she invites her readers to disabuse themselves of the romanticized descriptions of Africa which use the "man Friday", "Tarzan of the Apes", or the "noble savage" vocabularies and metaphors such as abound in official colonial histories, travelers tales and missionary journals.

The chief merit of this well-written little volume is its wealth of scholarship based on competent and judicious use of early Arab sources, and modern ethnographic, linguistic, and archeological evidence supported by insights derived from geography and ethno-botany. The author, however, uses her sources with scholarly caution; and while she studiously refrains from making exaggerated claims and sweeping categorical statements, she succeeds by the deftness and delicacy of her pen in removing the veil of darkness over this pre-colonial period of African history for English-speaking peoples. She also opens new windows and new chinks of light to illuminate for us the erstwhile dark corners of Africa's historical past. Thus, we get a clearer picture of the spread of Islam in West Africa and the role of the stringent apostles of that religion in the historic event. New light is also thrown on the dubious theory of Egyptian origins of African cultures.

The book also contributes to our understanding of the social history of the period. Thus, towns like the fabled Timbuktu become alive in these pages with descriptions of social life which check out with modern anthropological accounts which we have of the city. So, too, is the picture of Songhai enlivened by sociological details which give authenticity and an African flavor to the accounts.

The scholarly merit of this book is its "raison d'etre." However, it is important to point out that the book is timely for other reasons. First, it is well to remind ourselves of the international environment in which we live and of the fact that ever since Africa and her peoples were catapulted into the world scene as active participants just over a decade ago, we can no longer perpetuate the myth of yesterday. There is a growing need to close the information gap which has existed for so long in the West, and Mrs. Rosenthal's book is an important contribution in this respect.

In the second place, it is important for Americans, ten percent of whom are of African descent, to be well informed on the historical background of Africa and the Africans. It is, I venture to suggest, an exercise in self-understanding, for the ten percent of the American population has played no mean part in the economic and artistic developments of this country. It seems only proper that the historical background of the Afro-Americans should get the kind of proper and factual treatment usually accorded to the historical backgrounds of British, German, Italian or Greek Americans.

Absolom L. Vilakazi

School of International Service,
The American University
Washington, D.C.

I
The Study of African History

First, strip away the myth that Africa, South of the Sahara had no history before the coming of the Europeans in the 14th century. Tear up the roadway of African history that has been paved with the notion that what history Africa did have, was neither intelligible nor significant. The next task is to straighten out some of the pathways that were a detour on the road to understanding African history. To do this we must separate the early chronicles and their romanticized descriptions that suggest the "man Friday" and the "noble savage," from the official colonial histories. Only by breaking up the cement of traditional prejudices that have bound the whole study of Africa for centuries can we insure, once and for all the intellectual decolonization of the continent. This intellectual decolonization is in fact the freeing of students, teachers, and Africans themselves from the once all pervasive mentality of the colonizer.

As citizenships multiply, and the status of being a citizen is experienced by the peoples of the new nations, it is quite natural for them to see their future in more positive terms, and in that same spirit they will seek out their own past histories. The leadership in Africa is now in the act of redefining their past in terms of the present, and they are doing so, sometimes with anguish, but with the remarkable adaptability that they have shown throughout the centuries. We too, are in the same position that the young African students find themselves, we know of African-Negro history only through the eyes of the European, who either conquered them for economic reasons, or exploited them after a show of force, or pretended to have a civilizing mission in order to do just what the others did. In America the pernicious attitude that black Africa had no history, so therefore its descendents in America could have none, found an unquestioning audience. Removing that European backdrop, which is what is meant by intellectual decolonization, Africans are, for the first time seeking to learn their own history, which has been surreptiously spirited away by the colonial powers.

So pressing was the situation following independence in the 1960's of African teachers and students for authoritative textbooks on African history, that the Department of History at Ibadan University (Ibadan, Nigeria) conducted a workshop in March 1965. At that time a number of African historians presented papers on various themes, encompassing as large an areas as possible in a very short period of time. This high level seminar produced a kind of working classroom syllabus, responding as quickly as humanly possible to the demands for a truly African history. This in no way was to be a permanent working method for the amassing and systematizing of material, but, came in response to requests from the growing centers of learning in Ibadan, Zaria (northern Nigeria), Accra (Ghana), and Dar-es-Salaam (Tanzania); this demand must be met but cannot be adequately filled at the moment. With this marked acceleration there has been a freely moving traffic of ideas between Africa and Europe, and unfortunately to a lesser extent with the United States in this field.

The deadening concept that sub-Saharan Africa had no indigenious tradition of historical writing of its own, thereby being arid of any history, has been condemned to the dust heap forever.

African experts in America, always a precious few, have in the past tended to follow European thinking concerning the abilities and the cultural resources of the African peoples. It is said that because of the more openminded approach of American anthropologists, who stress the equality of mankind as a first principle in their work, that the more recent studies of African peoples have greater scope. Now that the history of sub-Saharan Africa is finally being reconstructed, and read critically, it has been found that it is for the most part a monument of elusive misconceptions solidly based on some of the traditional biases of some European scholars who dominated the thinking of their age. The lack of a written language

2

has led to the widely held assumption that no chronicles existed for the period of history which we are covering. This never had a basis in fact, the documents of the Timbuktu (Mali) school written in Arabic and of West African origin, form a restricted body of work along with the priceless sources of the Arab geographers and Leo Africanus from the 14th to the 16th century, which we are forced to draw upon so heavily. Much of the work of the Arab geographers is still unavailable in English. In modern Ghana, unknown works have been uncovered of the Gonja dynasty's conversion to Islam in the 16th century. Documents of African origin will prove to be a very important component in the future understanding of African history. Their value rests in having the African's view of his own society, rather than that of an outsider looking in. These original African documents will not only add facts that we need to know, but will most likely suggest the atmosphere in which people lived, and why particular things were important to them. The travels of Europeans in the 15th century and the mass of records kept by missionaries, traders and administrators when they become fully available will illuminate other aspects.

This book, written within the framework of the narrative, but in the spirit of scholarship, attempts, with the scant and scattered information at our disposal now, to view the West African medieval empires as being more than the plotting of battles, catastrophes, courts, assemblies, but as being part of human life, with unique modes of thinking, feeling and acting. I have sought to depict the customs and spirit of the times which really form the daily background of life, along with its intrigues and wars.

The life-history of the African has not only been distorted historically, but had also been undervalued culturally. In order for Europeans to enslave Africans in "good conscience" they had to discredit any abilities of theirs that might raise them to the status of men. It is no accident that the distinctiveness of African art, had been thought for generations to be of European origin. The beautiful Benin bronzes, made by the lost wax process, which only came to the notice of Europe in the late 18th century had always been thought to be of Portuguese origin. Re-

3

markable bronze heads have been found at a place called Ife. which is close to Benin in the forest belt of Nigeria. These pieces of sculpture have been tenatively dated as from 1000 A.D. to 1200 A.D. This dating is based in relation to an analysis made of the Nok figurines (Nok is a village in Northern Nigeria) made by the radiocarbon method at Yale University (Yale Natural Radiocarbon Measurements III) which has been dated at about 200 B.C. (or about 100 B.C. to A.D. 200 or 300).

It had always been thought that because of their contact with the Portuguese, who were in Africa about 1500 A.D. that, the African had learned this skill of bronze casting from them. No valid argument could be made for these figures being Portuguese, there were no comparable works of art in Portugal at that time. It is most certain that the Portuguese did not bring artists along on their explorations in order to teach the Negroes an art that has been recognized to be a very demanding one in its technique.

The dating of the Ife heads and the Nok figurines are not mere technicalities. What they point to is the fact that we can assume that there were well established traditions in the working of plastic art forms in West Africa before the peoples had any contact with Europe. Scientific evidence like that of the radiocarbon dating has finally freed us from the tyranny of how much time it takes to acquire the skill and competence to produce a masterpiece. For the Benin bronzes have proved their intrinsic worth!

The continuing inference that all influence stemmed from Egypt is now being seriously questioned. Professor Raymond Mauny, a French Africanist says that the evidence is "fragile." To note the further ferment in the field of African studies, scholars are disagreeing quite vehemently with the acknowledged authorities: Vincent Monteil in his book "L'Islam Noir," seriously takes issue with the accepted date for the breakup of the Ghana Empire, he says, "this date, referred to by everyone without discussion, is due to Maurice Delafosse who indicates nowhere the definite origins of the statement." In fact, most of the dates in this area of historical studies are "controversial" at this point.

Although the past twenty years have seen an upsurge of the work in African history, the Medieval West African Empires are still a subject of fascinating obscurity. The persistent myth that the modes of life which led to the building of empires came from the white peoples of North Africa or the Europeans is a controversial one. There are those that see the Western Sudan shaped by these outside forces stressing "whiteness," and introducing the racial factor. The impressions of early travelers to Benin, Ashanti (Ghana) and Dahomey seem to annihilate the racial and North African influence arguments. The non-Islamic peoples in the forest area all were found to have a lengthy prior tradition as highly organized states before the coming of Islam or the Europeans.

The traditions of the Ghana, Mali, and Songhai Empires is embedded so deeply in the history of the area, that the memory of their power and prestige could not be wrested from them in the 20th century—it is no mistake that Mali still retains her ancient name, and that Ghana was chosen to make a modern day reappearance.

II
African Empires—Ghana

First the Kente cloth seemed to fill the aisle of the General Assembly Hall. The woven silk of yellow, red, and black worn like a toga had captured everyone's attention on that day of September 23, 1960. Ghana had already made her entrance as an independent state on the world stage in March, 1957. This fact in no way extinguished the excitement of seeing the first President of Ghana, he then seemed so much an emblem of emerging Africa. The toga-attired man was Dr. Kwame Nkrumah, then Head of State. His appearance underscored the fact that his country was the first black African state to ascend the world platform following World War II. In modern day political terms, Ghana had become independent. Ghana had attained "the political kingdom," in the words of Dr. Nkrumah.

Ghana did not just begin her political life that day in the domed blue and gold hall of the United Nations. Every step of Dr. Nkrumah's towards the marble-green podium from where he was to address the assembled statesmen of the world must have been filled with great emotion. He must have felt keenly the mantle of history both present and past, that he carried upon his shoulders like the Kente that he wore. The predominantly yellow thread running through his silken costume could easily remind him of the historic gold trade that made ancient Ghana, first the name of a city, and later that of a kingdom, one of vast riches, which flourished while Europe was still in the dark ages. Africans in the Gold Coast, and British Togoland had shown by the choice of this name that they were not only gaining the present for themselves, but in fact repossessing the past glory that was surely theirs. The black thread could not help but signify the painful shadow of the European slave trade;

responsible for thrusting the history of a whole continent in the shade for Western man, the red could only be the terra-cotta of the African soil from which its whole being sprung.

It is certain that Ghana did not exist on the territory of modern day Ghana. Her roots go back to the first millenium A.D. The site of her beginnings, thought lost for all times by most historians, has been established and located by French archeologists at Kumbi Saleh, in Mauritania, or three hundred miles west south-west of Timbuktu. It was called Kumbi then. The kingdom was very old, and was said, according to Es-Sadi, a noted historian residing on the Niger Bend, at Timbuktu, to have had twenty-two kings before the Hejira (Mohammad's flight from Mecca), and probably just as many after. The ancient empire of Ghana at her height probably included the present states of Senegal, The Gambia, Mali, Guinea, and part of Mauritania.

When recorded accounts finally did appear, they were in the form of memorable descriptions written in the 11th century by Arab geographers, who either journeyed themselves to West Africa, or with equal persistence and passion studied the log books of explorers and the reports of the Barbary pirates. Barbary is a belt of country separating the Mediterranean from the Sahara Desert; it further extends from Tripoli in the east to the Atlantic Ocean in the west.

One such scholar was Abu Obeid El-Bekri, an Arab from Cordova in Spain and a student of North African history. Although this man, who came from a noble family, never set foot outside Spain, his pen left its imprint on a remarkable and diverse range of works from a survey of plants and trees of Andulusia, in his native Spain, to several volumes on general geography which have quenched the thirst of students of African history for centuries. El-Bekri must have been a man possessed of an immense curiosity, for he was the first Islamic scholar to give a general survey of the area of the Western Sudan. Sudan, means the land of the blacks, a translation from the Arabic, "Beled es Sudan," it is the acceptable term for the area approximately from the Red Sea to the Atlantic, including that part which lies to the west of Lake Chad. It is believed that El-Bekri had the use of the official archives of Cordova. This privilege was probably due to the influence of his family, which was a household of considerable importance in the early part of the 10th century in Spain. Copies of his geographical works, which have proved in later generations to have been of great accuracy, can be seen today in the Bibliotheque Nationale in Paris, and the British Museum in London. In fact, we owe all our knowledge of ancient African history to a hardy band of devoted Arab authors of which El-Bekri is only one. Some were travellers by nature, but all were industrious diarists.

These Arabs, made curious by the works of Ptolemy, which had been translated into Arabic by the Christian churches, apparently needed very little encouragement to undertake a voyage which would not be completed for years.

Masudi, the first of the Arabs to voyage out, was a citizen of Baghdad, who traveled some twenty years, his trips taking him to such far flung places as China and Madagascar. He was the first to record the unusual way in which the gold trade of the early Ghana Empire was carried on; a subject which will be explored later. Ibn Haukal, also from Baghdad, and a contemporary of Masudi can really be considered the first explorer of West Africa, and is believed, after seeing the Niger River flowing eastwards, to have confused it with the Egyptian Nile. Ibn Haukal mentioned black Africa only in passing, and it was concluded from that, that he felt that what he saw, was hardly worth recording.

Fortunately, the Arab scholars that followed him, such as El-Bekri, El-Edrisi, Yagut, El-Omari, Ibn Battuta and Ibn Khaldun, did not share his negative attitude.

Although we think of Africa, South of the Sahara, as being populated solely by dark-skinned people, the stories told of the empire in embryo have been tantalizing, but insecure in regards to its actual truth. For some time historians and specialists have been saying that the first rulers of Ghana were not only white but that they were of ancient Jewish stock. It is thought that Jewish groups who had rebelled against the Romans in Cyrenaica in 115 A.D. migrated to the Western Sudan by two different routes, one through Air (near Agades, placed in Niger) in the desert across the Niger Bend to the area of Senegal and Guinea. It was at this point that they were joined by the others who were taking a westerly route through southern Morocco and the Mauritanian Adrar mountains. These Jewish peoples inter-married with the pastoral Fulani, and it is said that the Fulani had carried these traits as far as Lake Chad. In the last few years, some rethinking has been taking place among historians and specialists in relation to the origins of Ghana. Although the theory of the Jewish tribes has lost some of its force, it is still stoutly maintained that the first rulers were white. A noted American anthropologist, whose work is widely respected, has felt that he must strip away this story through the use of the scientific methods at the disposal of modern day anthropologists. Professor Murdock says in his book, "Africa its Peoples and their Culture History," that it was the negroes, who also occupied the Western Sahara with the white skinned Berbers at about the same time who were the first rulers of Ghana . . . "It was these people and not some unidentified Caucasoid group as it is sometimes alleged, who formed the core of the great empire of Ghana."

It is impossible at this time to know in the light of the last analysis just what group was displaced; the king being assassinated brought the Soninke's into control of growing Ghana. This much is clear, that following the ascent to the throne by the Soninke, a branch of the Mandingo peoples, that Ghana began to extend her boundaries and influence. We are not precisely informed as to how the land area was extended, since there were no written records about these earliest times. Ghana had early contacts with North Africa, located as she was at the southern end of important caravan routes. Sijilmasa in lower Morocco (it no longer exists) was the transshipment point for both countries, indicating that the Sahara Desert, far from being a barrier, was rather a pathway between North Africa, and Africa South of the Sahara. Bustling activity between North, and Africa South of the desert is the picture we get from Ibn Haukal, in his description of Sijilmasa, which was founded in the 8th century A.D. This town of "middling size" he said was located near the gold mines. "These mines are said to be of the most pure and excellent gold; but it is difficult to work them, and the way to them is dangerous and troublesome." In this climate, which was said to be rather delightful, both Ghana and Morocco were trading gold and salt by way of what must be called some of the oldest highways in the world, the ancient caravan routes, both partners growing rich by this trade. Twice between 734 and 750 A.D. the Arab Moroccans launched attacks upon their wealthy trading partner, both were ineffective, and Ghana continued to maintain control over the gold producing areas.

Because of the constant cupidity in the hearts of men, Ghana did not experience the unhampered expansion of her territory or her influence. It was just about this time there arose a Berber Chief, called Tilutane, who came from a tribe called the Lemtuna, who lived in a town called Audoghast. Audoghast, locatable on the Mauritanian map today as a ruin, was said to have been in ancient times fifteen days march westward from the capital of Ghana. It is possible that Audoghast had been shuttled back and forth between the Berbers and the Ghanians. There is no doubt that it was a very desireable city at that time. Water was abundant (it is thought that the Sahara at one time had more rainfall than it experiences today),dates, millet, figs and vines along with cattle and sheep flourished. Wheat was grown there in small quantities. Wheat was always considered to be a great luxury and was for the most part an import with dried fruits, brass, clothing, salt, honey and gold.

It was no secret that Tilutane had grabbed Audoghast at least once from the Ghana king at some stage; there had been friction for some time between the Soninke and Lemtuna tribes. Interestingly enough, excavations carried out in 1960-61 have come upon what they think is the probable site (it never was definitely established) of Audoghast. Two completely different sets of ruins have emerged from the silent sands. This is perhaps the city that El-Bekri said was destroyed around 1055 A.D. A large medieval site, and in the middle of it a more recent one, has been uncovered. In it were found Atlantic shells. Along with this was some green enameled pottery, similar to other finds in West Africa. Certainty will come about after these objects have been dated scientifically by the radio-carbon method.

The king of Ghana was keenly sensitive to the encroachments of his neighbors, and was aware that Tilutane had a firm hold on all the Berber tribes in the Western Sahara, and his ambitions did not cease with that. Boundaries, as we have noticed, were not clearly fixed in those times, so one had to keep a sharp eye on one's outlying districts, where ties to the central authority were bound to be less effective. Tilutane's army was said to have consisted of 100,000 men mounted on camels, whom he put to use by ordering them to conduct raids on the outlying districts of the Ghana Empire.

These two powerful contenders never came to a confrontation, though it must have given the Lemtuna an unholy joy to know that they had managed to be successful in agitating the local politicans of the day by intervening in the agreements that Ghana had made with the vassal chiefs under her control. The king of Ghana did eventually recover the territory snipped off by the raiding Berber king, the Soninke then claimed Audoghast, but they never occupied it.

While Ghana flourished, the Western Sahara was in ferment, because of the conquests made by a fiery and austere teacher of Islam, Ibn Yacin. His doctrine of strict Islamic observance was met by such a violent reaction from the tribesmen at Jedala, where he first sought to preach, that they burnt his house to the ground and drove him out. This led him to isolate himself on an island in the Senegal River. People, being what they are, became so curious as to why he secluded himself, that many of the surrounding tribes sought out his teaching, and by that method he gained about 1,000 followers and named them Almoravids. The word Almoravid is really a distortion of a Spanish word meaning El-Morabetin, or the people of the monastery. His fiery personality and strong will urged him to go out and compel, by conquest if necessary, the rest of the world to accept his creed. In 1057 he died fighting. In 1100, the inheritors of Ibn Yacin's role stretched their conquests further. In 1076 the Almoravids captured Ghana, but it was not an easy victory, nor was it an empire that shattered quickly as we shall see.

Among El-Bekri's prodigious and remarkably accurate scribblings we find that the capital of the Ghana Empire was really composed of two parts or twin cities. One was called Kumbi, seemingly a Moslem town, and the other El Ghaba, which was considered to be the pagan quarter. Excavations made in the early 1900's had already shown, when the foliage and vines were torn away, that the hewn stones and pieces of ornamental sculpture were illustrative of the life of the area. Stone is not commonly used in Negro Africa simply because it is not available in any great quantities. It was more surprising to find that two-story houses were made of blocks of stone cemented together by mud. The digging also uncovered the fact that the walls were covered on the inside with some kind of colored plaster, which was used for decorative purposes. No doubt the piecing together of the early and the later excavations will add to our knowledge.

El-Bekri tells us that El Ghaba, the pagan quarter, was surrounded by a thicket, which was regarded as a sacred grove by the dwellers of this town. The thorny and dense underbrush was thought to house spirits important in the life of the people, and it was also said to be the place where the royal tombs were housed. Kumbi had no less than a dozen mosques scattered about, and was the home of many famous jurists and doctors of the time. As if to prove the quickening pace of African excavations and to corroborate the descriptions of El-Bekri, exciting discoveries have been made in the modern Koumbi Saleh in Mauritania, which revealed for the first time here the presence of several large tombs outside the city. Again well-built stone houses have been unearthed, but this time triangular niches were found in the wall and Koranic inscriptions on the plaster.

The method of spreading the Islamic creed among the black African was said to be fierce and merciless at times to those who did not succumb by persuasion to the teachings of Mohammad. The Ghana Empire, or the king, did not insist on acceptance of this new faith. El-Bekri noted a remarkable sense of religious equality there, as evidenced by the fact that both pagans and Moslems held office side by side.

Paganism in Africa is imperfectly understood. Living in a hostile environment, natural objects become quite sensibly the objects of veneration. There is the concept of the creator tied to what is called the descent group by the very virtue of having created the great ancestor. There is some belief in the after-life, and this is viewed as the extension of life itself. There is the belief in spirits, which are said to have the power of intervention in the world of the living. In order for man to mediate between himself and the deities there is an organized priesthood. These systems of belief can be very complex. Studies have found that the beliefs of some of the pagan forest peoples like that of the Dogan in Dahomey and the Nupe in Nigeria are highly organized logical systems, culminating in impressive philosophical insights.

The dust of centuries now covers the past glitter of what once was Kumbi, which according to El-Edrisi was the largest market in the Sudan due purely to its gold trade. If these Arabic scholars can be relied upon, and it has been proven for the most part how accurate they were, then the dust that has covered Kumbi, also covers its past glory all earned with gold dust.

So extensive was this trade due to its location at the southern end of the western caravan route, that it enabled the king of Ghana to rule over a court of great pomp and elegance. So abundant was the gold at that time that the price had to be controlled. Nuggets were considered to be crown property while the gold dust was used for trade. The king was said to have lived in such luxurious circumstances that even his horse was hitched to a gold nugget. El-Edrisi, a man who gave great luster to Arab science in the eyes of the Western world, first reported this. It has always been acknowledged that rumor had cast the nugget in a somewhat larger size, be that as it may, it was nevertheless an out-sized object. Ibn Khaldun says in his journal that a prince went on a spending spree and bought the nugget and sold it to some Egyptian merchants, and to answer all the former arguments as to its size, it did in fact weigh a ton!

It can hardly be said that descriptions of the court of Ghana abound, so we are grateful for El-Edrisi's account which fires the imagination while adding to the picture.

He refers to the king as the king of Tekrur, a small kingdom situated approximately in the vicinity of Senegal. Tekrur is probably a lot more important than anyone could know for there are a scattering of mysterious references in which Ghana is coupled with it. "A mightly Prince having many servants and soldiers, of known fortitude, power and justice with a country well secured and exposed to no fears." A city famous for "business and useful arts for the advantage of its people." El-Edrisi unhestiatingly labels the king as "The most just of all men." He is impressed with the pomp of the court describing how the king when he goes out, riding horseback, is rich with ornaments and marches with elephants, camels and other beasts. He also observes that when the king goes out he is brought cases to settle while he rides on horseback among his people, and it is here that he settles cases or disputes that are brought to him.

Although the king ruled over what was mostly an agricultural people who grew millet and fished, they also dined decently on wild game, it is said that their main preoccupation was the gold-salt trade which consumed the energies of the capital.

"I heard the sound of clapping," says El-Bekri in one of his descriptions taken from someone who had actually seen an audience with the Ghana king. "I tore my eyes from the person of the king, who was adorned in a headdress of gold, and other bright jewelry which was gold. Pages holding gold hilted swords and shields were on one side, and vassal princes wearing splendid ornaments on the other." Our viewer through his pen goes on to tell us that dogs guarded the entrance to the king's throne room and that they followed the monarch about trailing the noise of tinkling bells that were attached to their collars. "What was this clapping about?" Oh, interjects El-Bekri, that was found to be a sign of respect shown by Moslems for the king. The pagans threw dust on their heads for the same reason.

The Ghana Empire and its vast territory is said to have extended from the fabled Timbuktu (in Mali) in the east, to the upper Niger in the south-west, and in the west to the border of Tekrur. Everyone of importance in Europe was familiar by rumor, later confirmed by travellers that Ghana's immense wealth did not rest only upon copper, dried fruits and cowries. Cowries are small shells used for barter, obtained from the Indian Ocean, and were a symbol of fertility and wealth. It was the source of the gold that was sought after. It was known that the king did not control the area from which it was mined. The question that was on everyone's lips was, "Why was it traded in such a secret manner?" It was later learned that a people called Wangara mined the gold. In order to acquire this precious metal, Ghanian merchants were forced to take a twenty day trip across the burning Sahara to a spot near the Senegal River where "men lived in holes," these obviously were the gold mines. The merchants had found from experience that the Wangarans refused to see strangers. So, weary as the travellers were, they were obliged to place their wares on the ground, and then withdraw from sight. The miners in turn crept out of hiding to see if the quantity of salt, jewelry, and the supply of resinous wood (used for flavoring water) carried in animal skins was acceptable to them. If this was so, they put a mound of gold dust beside the goods of the merchants. If this bargain was sealed, the merchants signaled by beating a drum (or a deba as it is called), then the market was concluded. This arrangement was known as "dumb barter." Curiosity once reached such a point that some of the merchants actually captured one of the shy Wangaran people. It was said that he pined away and died without ever unsealing his lips. The Wangarans kept this secret for fear that they would be invaded if found out. They kept up this brisk trade due to their desperate shortage of salt.

The location of the gold fields of the Wangara has never been solidly identified, and it is a puzzle that has vexed the minds of the Moors, engaged the armies of the Moslems and Europeans up until the nineteenth century. Sifting through the accounts of centuries, the mines appear to be in the vicinity of Senegal, in fact near the Senegal River. It would seem that leaf upon leaf of confusion has been laid upon the mystery of the location of one of the best kept secrets in history. Evidence to date leans towards a place called Bambuk-Bure which was not far from Kumbi. It is very likely that these gold fields were included in the Ghana Empire, or they were considered to be directly under the control of the king. Edrisi declared that Wangara was located upon an island surrounded by waters. This island was flooded and when the water receded the gold was collected. The topography of Senegal, with its series of broken-up lands within it, fills that description remarkably well.

Ibn Battuta, the traveler of Islam, and Leo Africanus centuries later, confirmed this description. Hemmed in by four rivers, the Senegal on the north, the Faleme on the west, and on the east by the Niger, and on the south by The Tinkisso, it would appear that this is indeed the spot of the mythical but highly productive gold fields. The riddle of the location of these gold mines was almost solved to satisfaction in 1550. It seems that a Portuguese managed, no doubt with great difficulty, to reach Bambuk. At this time the gold fields were producing their utmost. Strangely enough he left no account of himself or what he found there. We had to wait for three centuries for the era of European exploration. Both the Scottish explorer Mungo Park, and the Frenchman René Caillié discovered gold fields on the upper Niger River, but so overworked were the mines that it did not occur to the explorers to pin the legend to any sort of truth. Amazingly enough, it was found in the nineteenth century that the gold then flowing into Morocco was referred to as Wangara gold.

Today the silent trade is as silent as it is ever going to be, it is gone along with the depletion of the mines. Accurate present day accounts say that gold is still washed down from the Faleme River and its branches in Senegal. Gravels once fantastically productive, although worked to the point of exhaustion are said to revive, when allowed to lie fallow for several years.

Arabs and Africans alike had heard of this silent trade and the strange ways of the Wangarans. It was common knowledge that the whole mining operation was controlled by priests or people who practiced the art of witchcraft. Trading without talking had taken place before in the history of the world. The historian of the ancient world, Herodotus, gave a similar description of how gold was bartered among the Carthaginians. We are also told that silk was traded in just this way in the Himalayas in days of old, and that it had been described by a Chinese explorer who had noted its occurrence in Ceylon in the 15th century.

Although the principal item of trade, for the merchants of North Africa, was gold, there was a hectic traffic in slaves, a very saleable commodity. Slavery, and its African and European connotations are quite different. For present purposes it is necessary to note that in West Africa, just as it was in the early history of Europe, slavery was quite common. Negroes became slaves if they were captured as a result of a battle, or suffered the fate of being a slave due to the non-payment of debt, or else might have been enslaved as a punishment for a crime. Historians and geographers say that since the conversion of the people of North Africa to Islam, that the traffic in black slaves increased. No Moslem by law could enslave another, so that the Negroes who were not Moslems were in great demand in the North African market place. Slaves in a Moslem household were in fact domestic slaves or more accurately domestic workers, and at times became part of the family. They did not suffer the personal cruelties that were later on characteristic of the European slave herders who captured them for use on the plantations of the United States and the West Indies.

The fact that the majority of the people of the Ghana Empire resisted the influence of Islam was a cause of great anger to the Almoravids. Tales of how the king of Ghana, enthroned on a seat of gold, surrounded by flaming torches while having his thousands of subjects served dinner, must have made their blood boil. The existence of this pagan empire to the south of them could not go undisturbed or unchallenged. The Almoravids continued to spread Islam by force of arms. After the death of Ibn Yacin in 1057, the Almoravids elected a spiritual leader, but he died soon after his appointment, and power became clenched in the fist of Abu Bakr. By this time the Almoravids were anything but a unified group, and there were many persons vying for power, as there always is after the death of a leader. Abu Bakr managed to unify the warring factions. Restlessness now gripped his tribesmen, who were nomads and used to moving from place

to place. Before handing over the reigns to his nephew
Yusuf, he unleashed a campaign against the Soninke, whose
king was known to be friendly to the Moslems . . . such
are the ambitions of men! There was no open war with
the Ghana Empire at this time. Meanwhile, Abu Bakr
who had surrendered the command of the northern Berber
army to Yusuf, burned with personal ambition while
spreading the word of Islam by the sword. He found an
ally in the king of Tekrur. This alliance eventually brought
the downfall of the great Ghana Empire under the Almoravid forces of Abu Bakr, and brought too, the downfall of the city. Sixteen years before Ghana's downfall
the king fought valiantly and placed some 200,000 warriors, including 40,000 archers, in the field in an effort
to retain her freedom. "So fell," wrote Ibn Khaldun, a
scholar of the 13th century, "one of the greatest and
most populous cities of the world."

With the death of the Berber leader Abu Bakr in
1087, the Almoravids fell apart as a unified group. At
this time the remains of the Ghana Empire tried to pull
itself together. The territories that had united to make it
great, like Tekrur, at least as an ally, had betrayed the
king, they were no longer willing to obey a central authority, so Ghana failed to recover from the fatal blow struck
by the Almoravids.

One of the vassal states once ruled by Ghana was the
kingdom of SuSu (or SoSo). This kingdom became a
refuge for those of the Soninke people who had escaped
the massacre that had taken place in the Ghana capital.
In 1203 the SuSu felt that they were strong enough to
take over what was left of the old Ghana Empire. King
Sumanguru's reign in Ghana was not a success and
deepening dissatisfaction led the Arab merchants to pack
their belongings in 1224, and under the spiritual leadership of a Sheikh from Mecca moved 100 miles north of
Ghana. They set up a home upon what was once the
camping ground for caravans. The town was called Walata,
and it prospered.

Robbed and stripped of its former greatness—Ghana
was completed blotted out. The Akan peoples of present
day Ghana, who live in the savanna-forest area, like to

think that they are descended from those peoples who refused to become Moslems.

The kingdom of Mali (or Melle or Mande) was conceived and commanded on a grander scale than that of its predecessor, Ghana. Mali at its apogee could boast of being ruled by one of the most enlightened rulers of its time, plus the fact that he was one of the great showmen of his day.

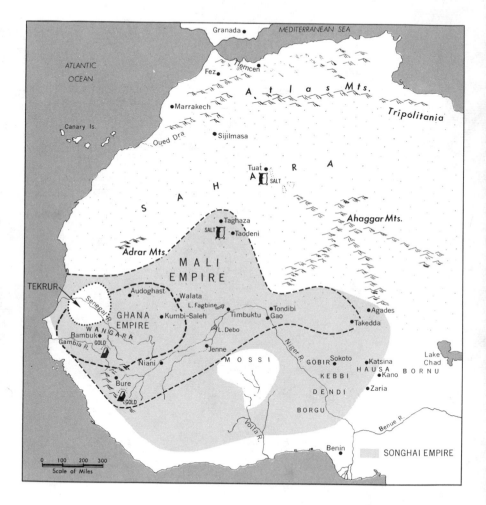

III
African Empires—Mali

It is in the spirit of the upward and outward curve of the renowned antelope sculpture of the Upper Niger, whose region the growing Mali Empire was to gradually embrace, that the kingdom of the Mandingos, a branch of the Soninke rulers of Ghana, can be understood. Mali or the Malinke, as they are called, expanded upward and outward far beyond the territorial claims of ancient Ghana. At one time she encompassed all the land along the Niger as far as Gao, reaching upward into the Sahara desert as far as the vital salt mines of Taghaza, and the copper mines of Takedda. Curving westward she conquered lands into Senegal and the Gambia; adding at this time the precious gold mines, the location of which had eluded Europeans for centuries, and whose existence is being clarified today as more and more intensive research is carried out. Some specialists stretch the eastern reaches of Mali as far as the Hausa city-states of Kano, Katsina, and Zaria, all still existing as important centers of Islam today in northern Nigeria. Neither the topography nor the texture of the life of these former city-states differ markedly today from that of their past. Neither the Mossi states in the southeast, nor Tekrur, non-existent today, near Senegal were part of that empire. Tekrur's history eludes us, but for the fact that we know that this kingdom was converted to Islam in the first half of the 11th century. The kings of Mali were known in Egypt as the kings of Tekrur, which seems to shroud further the mystery, wrapping it as it does, in those inevitable mists and vapors that cling so persistently to the west coast of Africa. Interestingly enough, the French administrative unit known as the Federation of Mali in the 20th century closely approximated the Mali Empire. The empire included all of the state of Mali as we know it today, part of Niger perhaps, a sliver of Upper Volta pushing right up to the frontier of Guinea and taking in Senegal and the Gambia.

It is impossible before the 13th century to plot the origin of this growing power of Mali which was a small Sudanese kingdom on the upper Bakhoy which was gradually extending eastward. It was expanding enough to strike jealousy in the hearts of its neighbors. One such neighbor was the SuSu king, Sumanguru, who, flushed with his successful capture of Ghana, or what was left of it after her military defeat at the hands of the Berber Almoravids, was determined to halt the momentum of Mali which was already showing signs of commercial success. What was particularly annoying to the SuSu, who had never converted to Islam, was the respect and prestige being garnered by the ruling family for their strict observance of the Hadj, or the pilgrimage that all Moslem believers take to Mecca. This carefully observed religious rite to the holy city carried with it, in its train, the benefits of friendships and the fruits of cultivated contacts accumulated as a result of such a time-consuming and arduous journey. These pilgrimages, to a great extent, stimulated the passage of ideas as well as of people. Time and patient unbiased research will show that these societies were as varied as the geography of the empire of Mali itself, stretching as it did from the harsh desert with its uncompromising sun, to the water-poor grass steppes folding into the lush savannas, then dipping into the steamy and seemingly velvetized heat that clutches the forest floor with its mangrove swamps around which raffia palms luxuriated.

If the quill of El-Omari, an Arab born in Damascus in 1301 had failed to make its geographical compilations, or if the energy of the theologian Ibn Battuta had flagged, or the interest of his scholarly contemporary Ibn Khaldun had abated, we would know practically nothing of this period of history in the Western Sudan. Ibn Battuta was the first to give an eye-witness account of travels in this area through his diary. El-Omari, when reaching adulthood took a post with the Sultan of Egypt, in 1132 he decided to resign this position and left Cario to pursue more seriously his life long interest in geography. This was to consist, in its final form, of oral and written accounts grouping themselves under the heading of educated compilations. It is from El-Omari's pen that we can get a glimmer of the reach of the Mali Empire. He assessed from his information that it took four months journey each way. Piece by piece we must view this past history as a vast mosaic of whose design we are just becoming aware, of which direct information is fragmentary. As one anthropologist has said, for every ton of earth about the Nile that has been excavated and analyzed, an ounce of the Niger has to stand nervously as an equal.

It is with the help of the Arab geographers that we have gained insight into the customs and spirit of the times. There is enough material here to fell once and for all the myth that there was no civilization in black Africa.

Ibn Battuta in 1352, many years after El-Omari had been in Cairo, began his travels in the Western Sudan. Setting out from Sijilmasa, non-existent today, thought to have been on the desert fringe in lower Morocco, he made his way to Walata, and from there it took twenty-four days to get to Niani, the capital of Mali, a town that does not exist today either. Walata in the desert, and Jenne on the upper Niger were handling most of the trans-Saharan trade at that time which had originally flowed through Ghana. The legendary city of Timbuktu on the Niger bend to the east, was already showing signs of burgeoning greatness.

We learn through these Arab diarists that Sumanguru, the SuSu king, failed to challenge successfully the power of Mali in 1235, by what must have seemed to him one of the unkinder cuts of fate.

Sundiata, the twelfth heir to the throne of Mali had been allowed to survive Sumanguru's sword due to the fact that he was a crippled child with a rather hopeless future. Reaching adulthood, Sundiata physically recovered from whatever affliction he had, and harboring no murky fears of his cruelly efficient neighbor, he struck a fatal blow at the envious SuSu kingdom, and in 1240 engulfed what was left of Ghana, just a fragment of this Negro non-Islamic empire that had flourished for 1,000 years.

Sundaita's first concern was to move the capital of Mali from a town called Jeriba to Niani. The city of Jeriba was also known as Mali or Mande; ruins have been found to indicate its existence. Archeological excavations show that Mani-Koura and Kangaba could have been the capital at any given time in the growth period of this great empire. Sundiata had no taste for war, but rather saw his role in the expansion of Mali as part of a monumental effort to unify and develop what was under his control and influence. This is comparable to the task set by all Africans on the continent in the 20th century, that, through the Organization of African Unity (OAU), the varied peoples of the continent can be drawn together.

Sundiata's mind increasingly dwelled upon embellishing his widening circle of influence with the grandeur of economic accomplishment. Word of the wealth of the empire persisted in Europe. It was learned that while the emperor controlled the sources of the gold production, the pagan diggers were not willing to be absorbed by him. Eventually, Sundiata did acquire adequate control over these sources to call them his own, and he did gain the much wished for control over the caravan routes to North Africa. The gold laborously delivered across the desert became the mainstay of the economies of medieval Europe. These medieval caravan trade routes go back to the first millenium B.C. This has been verified by the existence of the Sahara rock paintings, depicting horse-drawn chariots and indicating that there were means of transportation. Ground formations in the area are said to be trails worn by the foot-steps of men.

Although Mali controlled the production of the Wangaran gold fields, they, like their predecessors of the Ghana Empire, could not force the miners to work; the miners chose their own time and pace. It is thought, that in their contacts with the Wangara, that the Islamic peoples from the grass country were not altogether comfortable in the deep forests, and so they made no effort to force these pagans to trade the comforting spirits of the forest for Islam. Sundiata died after a 25 year reign, and during that time, despite his abhorrence for war, his generals stretched the empire and by the time of his death he had firmly established a dynasty. He was succeeded by his son Mansa (Mansa means Sultan) Ule.

Sundiata's generals even after his death were still unwilling to lay aside the mantle of military power and settle down as petty kings and rulers of small districts, as Mansa Ule would have preferred. Sundiata's son also showed no taste for war.

Mansa Ule was followed by four kings of whom we know nothing. About this time a surprising thing happened . . . a freed slave of the royal household grabbed the reigns of empire and proclaimed himself Emperor, Sakura was his name. Sakura had obviously observed and learned the strategems of emperors, and proved how successful the lesson can be learned by launching a palace coup with lightning success. It was through his efforts that Mali extended in breadth and purpose, experiencing commercial success also.

Sakura reigned for fifteen years, and although he was not a member of the original dynasty (Keita) of Mali, he too, was a devout Moslem, and longed to make a pilgrimage to Mecca. This he did, and on his way back, which was uneventful as far as we know, he avoided the customary route which ordinarily passes through Cario. For some unexplained reason he returned by way of Axum (an ancient settlement in Ethiopia) and came by way of the eastern Sudan (now Sudan). There, he debarked on the coast of then Somaliland and was assassinated by the Danakil. So sunk into the crystalline waters of the east African coast the slave Sakura.

Mali had not yet attained full stature; it was left to the grandson of Sundiata, Mansa Musa, a great showman and a man who had a emperor's drive for the dramatic who proved to be the most splendid and accomplished of the Mandingo Emperors. He came to the throne just fifty years after his grandfather's death.

The bazaars of Cairo could not be quieted—the least bit of gossip sprints from market to market stall in record time under any condition. There was no doubt about it, something extraordinary had captured the attention of that great city which served as an important caravan terminus. Reports of Mansa Musa's entrance into Cairo in 1324, seventeen years after his ascent to the throne was nothing short of spell-binding. For his own part,

Mansa Musa was on his way to the holy city of Mecca. It was said that when this remarkable sight came into view that 60,000 men were counted, including a personal retinue of 12,000 slaves, dressed in the most sumptious silks and brocades. This must be war, people thought, as 500 slaves each carrying a staff of gold weighing about 6 pounds were observed, and later this was noted down. This was an invasion surely—word darted from person to person! When the curtain of dust that had enveloped the caravan had cleared, it was learned that there was a baggage train of 80 camels carrying 300 pounds of gold dust each. The guardians of the caravan let this be known among the townspeople.

This was no invasion—impressions clarified, the air was clearing amid coughs and sneezes, but no violence was taking place, so fear was brushed aside as quickly as the handkerchief could remove dust from the eyes. It was learned that there was nothing to fear, no secret could be kept within the confines of the caravan for long. Word circulated through the market and wound round through the cool alleys where small artisans and their shops seemed to be in a cave, so sheltered were they from the sun, that this grand visitor was Mansa Musa! Such good behavior, such fine clothes—and they the citizens of Ciaro were well prepared to judge these refinements! This must be the caravan of a rich man, perhaps a Moslem, oh joy! it was learned he was also a pious Moslem. They could not know that this man was to elevate the city of Timbuktu to the point where it would become a great center of Islamic culture. It was difficult for those, that observed him that day, to know what aspirations this man had among this finery; for in fact, they had very little actual knowledge or contact with the "country of the black people" which is what the Sudan means.

Mansa Musa had no political motives, oh! relief! word swept through the city. Where had he come from was the question of the day. This immense caravan had made its way from Niani on the upper Niger to Walata, to Tuat, and then to Cario. Such a lengthy journey crossed the unrelieved dunes of the Sahara, with danger from many points from marauders. The boredom and beauty of this vast desert were part and parcel of this caravan.

The very name Sahara, legendary as a lure to men of all races, is an Arabic word symbolizing wilderness or emptiness, the word having the hot sound of a man gasping for breath. What these travellers endured, the terrible monotony, broken by chance once in a while by the fleeting hooves of the scimitar-horned Oryx! With the end of the day's heat, as surely came the sudden cold of the desert night. The nights in the desert have a virtue of their own. Brilliant night skys seem to remove the haze of fine dust that half obscures the merciless daytime sun. This caravan, like many others, must have camped gratefully near the spiky desert date (Balanites aegyptiaca) huddling near the lines of doum palms (Huphaene thebaica). These oases of rest are almost sacred to the traveller. These patches of green growth in the desert are designed by the whim of nature. When the rare, but awesome rain storm falls, water collects in hollows and watercourses and soaks into beds of silt and sand. It is here that the perennial plants and trees can live and man can take his respite—Mansa Musa felt such a journey worth it in the performance of his religious duties.

He could not stop in Cairo, for he must complete his religious devotions. He was slightly standoffish, and it was only through the persistence of his advisers that he called at all upon the Sultan of Egypt.

It was of this journey that El-Omari, 12 years later, heard in Cairo. It was through a conversation that he had had with a lawyer, that we learn that Mansa Musa described the length and breadth of his country as a year's journey across. It was more sensibly ascertained that it could have been four months journey each way. This state pilgrimage literally put Mali on the map. A map made in Majorica in 1331 by one Abraham Cresques, pictures Rex Melli, "the king of the gold mines."

Mansa Musa's veritable army of people, some for protection, others taken along for political reasons, also included doctors, chiefs, servants and family. This massive entourage caused so much gold to be put in circulation, that El-Omari's ears rang from the complaints of how the price of everything had gone up since the visit of that splendid and pious emperor. He was always referred to in a most respectful manner, though a conversation concluded with a complaint. Mansa Musa's charitable nature caused him to distribute gifts of gold in the holy cities, sending the price of this precious metal plunging.

Completing his religious duties in Mecca, his mind became restless. He felt that he must do something that would add to the splendor of his empire. Yes, he would do it, by some miracle he persuaded Es-Saheli, known as the poet-architect of Granada to accompany him home. Following this accomplishment, he received a message that Gao had been captured. Gao, a strategically located town had risen from Berber beginnings, and at that time was ruled by the Lemta Berbers; a people who had been driven out of Tripolitania (in Libya) by the Arabs. This was the first mention of Gao, a city of the Songhai people. The Songhai who had not always been Moslems, subsequently converted to Islam. The capture of Gao extended the Mali Empire for a thousand miles. Overjoyed by this news he was determined to visit this new captive of his on the middle Niger. This he did. His first task upon reaching Gao was to be received by the Songhai king, and to make sure of his loyalty. Although Mansa Musa was not known to be a cruel man, he was clever in the arts of empire building. He decided then and there that he did not trust the Songhai king, and that in order to insure his loyalty, or rather to diminish his influence, that he was going to take the king's two sons back to Niani (located close to Segu, which exists today). In time to come the Songhai would rise to greatness, but this was Mali's moment.

Gao, he noted, had no buildings really suitable, at least to his eye, for the worship of God. Who could he trust he thought, smiling to himself. Who, possessed the appropriate artistic sense, who possessed a cultured enough mind for such an important task? He knew the answer, of course; Es-Saheli could be entrusted with the task. Es-Saheli was eminently successful in behalf of his patron, he built Mosques of burnt brick, using the crenelated wall and enhanced the design of the roof with a pyrimidal minaret. He also designed several receiving houses for the king when he was in residence. This architecture was extended through the Western Sudan, where heretofore only cylindrical huts with conical roofs had been built. This style of architecture was admired as late as the 17th century. It is the famous Sankore Mosque in Timbuktu that is representative of that form.

Traveling with Mansa Musa was a rich merchant from Cairo. This is how he came to have this guest. It was inevitable that Mansa Musa should run out of gold. His generosity, alas! had overflowed into lavishness, and a steady depletion of funds followed. In Cairo he was forced to borrow money from a merchant. This man was not only skeptical but curious as to Mansa Musa's destination; and being only familiar by rumor with the interior of West Africa, he went with him. If the truth were to be known, payment of the debt was probably uppermost in his mind. This merchant's curiosity was probably more alive than the man himself, and the journey under the fierce and compelling sun was probably too much for him, and he died at Timbuktu. This was by no means the close of the transaction. The Emperor upon his arrival home sent a special courier across the desert to the man's children in Alexandria. With the money, he sent a greeting.

Located on the Niger buckle, which is a great curve of the Niger River, Timbuktu lived up to all the qualifications of its time-honored legend. The noise of its market place was positively deafening, not to mention the stimulating effects provided by this crossroads, where Tuareg, Arab, and Songhai met. Grain and kola nuts, whose entwining kernels, symbolizing friendship or solidarity are still valued today. Dates and fabrics rapidly changed hands too, the cloth sometimes being used as payment. But one of the greatest currencies was the exchange of ideas that passed from patron to patron.

Timbuktu had extensive caravan connections reaching all the way to Egypt. These wide connections emanating outward were the realization of Mansa Musa's dream. The city became a center of commerce and culture, one naturally enriching the other. The University of Sankore in Timbuktu was to become the nucleus of learning for the whole Middle East. With its great riches gathered from trade, its prestige was spreading and reaching the ears of the learned men of Walata. Word spread that the city was gathering around it an important core of scholars. Learned theologians, well versed in the Koran, and men of letters were gravitating to this city on the Niger—such was the intellectual ferment there! The city produced one eminent scholar, Professor Ahmed Baba, a great historian, much quoted in the "Tarikh-Es-Sudan," a collection of papers, published by the University of Sankore, and thought to have been edited in 1640.

Timbuktu today is just a small town in the north of the independent state of Mali. Her new life might be seen like that of the desert plant whose seeds lie dormant for years, waiting for adequate rain to set in motion an astonishingly rapid growth. The city, still a spot of fusion where Arab and Negro peoples meet, is again a germinating area.

Since its 20th century emergence Mali has discovered as part of its inheritance a vast amount of manuscripts in Arabic. Little known research undertaken under the guiding hand of the United Nations Educational Scientific and Cultural Organization (UNESCO) in Timbuktu, has discovered that there are private libraries that were unknown until recently. A UNESCO mission in 1964 managed to obtain access to some of these unique manuscripts. A 480 page manuscript unearthed by a Syrian research worker found that one ancient document contained information about a leading figure deeply involved in the history of Africa, a great scholar and religious leader of the Quadiriyya Order, his name Abu Bakr al-Kunti who lived from 1743 to 1826. It is thought now, that some preliminary research has taken place by this agency of the United Nations, that there are numerous documents recalling the history of the old civilizations of the Western Sudan, its scholars, its kings, and holy places. These manuscripts have been piled up in tents and stored in clay houses. They have been exposed to the vagaries of the weather, some no doubt by now injured by wind, sand ,and dust. An inventory of these private libraries has been far from complete. It is said to be a very delicate operation, more in line at times with diplomacy, for these books belong to old families who resent intrusions. So, the treasures of the old world are beginning again to flower in Mali, the new state.

In 1513 one Al Hasan ibn Muhammad Al Wazzan Al-Sayyato, more popularly known as Leo Africanus, visited the Sudan with his uncle, then on a diplomatic mission for the Sultan of Morocco to Askia the Great. The young man, then in his twenties, later wrote in detail of the atmosphere of Timbuktu. The encouragement for the writing down of these observations arose from a strange set of events.

While still in his twenties he was kidnapped by Sicilian pirates and handed over to Pope Leo X, who baptized him Leo. Pope Leo had heard from him of his strange and various travels and persuaded him to record them. This is how later the name of Leo Africanus became attached to this young man, and we are deeply grateful to him for his impressions. His diary or papers show that he was favorably impressed by the "influence of the merchants and intellectuals in the community." He recorded this in Italian, in a work called "The History and Description of Africa." His writings show that in this city there were judges, doctors and clerics, who flourished. They were all regarded highly, and received good salaries from the king. The intense respect for learning, says Leo, causes a heavy demand for books so "that more profit is made from the book trade than any other line of business."

One chronicler embellished his description of the intellectual climate of the city by enlivening it with an illustration. Once, he tells, Mansa Musa invited a famous lawyer to teach there. This lawyer upon his arrival went immediately to the university, the result of his visit was that he disqualified himself from teaching there. Rather, he said, I will go to Morocco and study several years more, and then return.

Mansa Musa died in 1332, no doubt with a feeling of great accomplishment. His son Maghan succeeded him, and it was in the four years, a short reign really, that this young man ruled, that Mali started to slip down from greatness. There is some indication, given by Ibn Khaldun, that a family struggle was taking place between Maghan and his uncle for the throne. His uncle Mansa Sulayman should have ascended the throne, being the eldest male in the family, and there is a suspicion that he was really deposed by his nephew. Aside from the palace family quarrels the kingdom was suffering from the raids of the Mossi warriors of Yatenga on the Upper Volta. Military defeats encouraged a laxity in Maghan, and in a fit of carelessness allowed the two hostage sons of the Songhai king (of Gao) to escape. They fled to their home, hoping to regain their independence.

If Mansa Musa's uncle, Sulayman, had not succeeded Maghan, whether he had deposed him or not now was immaterial, the empire would have further deteriorated. In the interim Gao had proclaimed its freedom as a result of Ali Kolen's escape, a bitter blow to Mansa Sulayman who had great difficulties in reasserting his authority over areas that had been moving out of his orbit since the Mossi raids. The Mossi, incidentally, never sought territorial expansion in these forays of theirs.

As the weight of empires preoccupies an Emperor, so must the burden of the ordinary day weigh differently upon the shoulders of the local populace. What sustains them, and in turn sustains the Empire, are the daily transactions of the markets whose picture can re reconstructed when we move closer to a portion of that day.

The sun rises after the darkness of the seasonal rain. The narrow room is enclosed by sand-clay bricks, narrow only because its construction is limited by the size of palm trunks, which are used for supporting the mud-matted palm fronds, which are laid over the beams to form a second story of the roof. One house looks much like another, though life is hardly monotonous. The room is a chokingly airless room; a woman awakes, it is late already, perhaps seven o'clock, already the market has begun to prepare itself for the days round of business. She opens a wooden door for relief from the heat, she is surrounded by the sudden coolness that has swept this land which is in drought all but two months of the year.

A neighbor is repairing his clay house, which is part of a never-changing necessity that the climate enforces. The rain, when it comes, washes away the outer coating of the bricks that make up the rectangular houses, closeted by a wooden door. When the torrential rain does come, and the split palm trunks, which do service as drains, overflow, there is not too much to repair, for the inner bricks are still intact.

Everyone in Timbuktu feels rewarded by the rains, it is a relief from the scorching sun, and the bleached board-like earth whose surface is only varied by foliage bordering the river. When it rains the earth comes to life and helps to sustain the flocks of goats and sheep that must live from the edible grasses. The semi-arid steppe, as it is called by geographers, can support a remarkable number of animals, even under the fierce sun and low rainfall. Close observers of the parched soil after a rain will be rewarded by the sight of a small lily-like plant that seems to spring from the soil. The temperature hovers between 100 and 110 degrees in the shade, and makes no daring plunge at night, but twindles to 90 degrees. The inevitable storms in August and September always come as a surprise, for they arrive without warning.

The market-women, the sellers in the market, hurry for cover when they see a dull orange cloud, which when recognized is sharply defined against the sky. It skuds overhead followed by a whirling dark cloud which casts a spectral light upon the ground below. The air inside the houses is stifling, fifteen minutes later when the chill rain comes down in torrents, clothesless children fight for a place beneath the palm-trunk drains. For a moment the market is like a lake, and then the glare of the sun returns. It is the official winter season here, for it is cool and it is time for the arrival of the great winter caravans, which arrive from the central Sahara with their precious slabs of salt, sometimes bringing exceptionally high prices. Books and manuscripts are always part of the caravan, along with a plentiful supply of manuscripts of the Koran. Included too are cloth, spurs, bridles, and other commodities. If the king is in residence at the time of the caravan's arrival, and hears that a horse has come into the city, he has the owner summoned, and pays a very high price for the animal, if the owner will sell . . . they are highly prized beasts!

It is in the northern part of the city that the caravan unloads. It is here they stay while the camels recuperate for several months; staying together in semi-permanent dwellings, and staying together for safety's sake. Here at at the northern edge of the city is where the Tuareg (a mixture of Berber and Negro) raid the incoming caravans with great profit.

The much waited for salt, mined at Taodeni, has unfortunately for the slave class of Timbuktu a villainous connotation. Men of their "class" worked these mines in the blinding and searing sun, where the temperatures could be nothing short of killing. With their legs in salty water, and only a brackish liquid to drink, many died. Such were the aspects of this society which had its own class distinctions.

There is little doubt that the rhythm of life is accelerated throughout the entire city when a caravan arrives. The hub of the area's activities and its influence radiates out for about a thousand miles. It is a spot of contact, and sometimes of conflict. The business of a market center such as Timbuktu was hardly a hodge-podge. The mixture of color and sound, fighting with the smells of the butcher's stalls is just a sign of an intricate economic structure.

As the market day opens, there is generally an early morning consensus as to the price of the much needed commodities. In some markets it is the first woman who arrives that sets the price. It is said that once the price is set, that it holds for the day, though it may fluctuate from day to day. The kind of sale by the "elbow" as sometimes cloth is sold, is subject to bargaining. When cloth is bought, as it might be, or used in small purchases as a medium of exchange, it was measured from the fingertips to the elbows. This can develop the most extraordinary controversaries. Bargaining is still the art, sport and hard business of the market. Leo Africanus described the "gentle and cheerful" temperament that breaks through in the course of a bargain. Unsuspecting strangers are sometimes cheated, and dishonesty was not punished, but there was a way of revoking a transaction if trickery was involved.

An air of sociability pervades the market, but this in no way declares that there is absolute trust between seller and buyer. Customary market practice was to use cowries (small shells from the Indian Ocean) for smaller purchases, and gold for the payment of larger transactions. The protocol was that the cowries were to be put in a basket alongside the goods being sold, the cowries could not be touched until the goods were actually taken by the purchaser. Wood-sellers, water-sellers, milk vendors, tailor's services, along with rice, millet, guinea corn, shea butter and kola nuts are hawked, and the sounds fill one's ears to the point of annoyance. The Tuareg herd supplies hides and dates and tobacco which are brought from Tuat. The sun eventually starts to take its toll. Those vendors who have their wares on matting in the market shift with the sun. Others become drowsy with the heat, and through the lessening noise one can catch the chanting of prayers. With the growing darkness, the day closes.

Timbuktu aspired to, and had every right to be called a great city. It had great differentiation both in politics and religion, it had a very specialized economy, and intellectuals living side by side with those who could not read or write. It is what present-day sociologists would call a "pre-industrial" city, and compares favorably with others cities at that stage of development.

Ibn Battuta, that tireless traveler of Islam of the 14th century, describes the Empire of Mali first hand for us. His records are spiced with a dash of annoyance, but this happens only occasionally.

He arrived in Niani, the capital of Mali, in June, after an exhausting journey of two months, spending much of the time mending and refilling precious water skins. Nomads added to the danger of caravan travel. It was their habit to hide the widely spaced desert wells by covering them with goatskins fixed to a wooden frame, and then in turn covering that with sand. This made the precious water holes indistinguishable from the rest of the sand. His caravan took him to Sijilmasa in lower Morocco through Taghaza, and he was greatly relieved to arrive in Walata, after having been lost in the desert with always the fear of perishing right there, never to complete his mission for Abu Inan (who seized the throne from his own father in Morocco). The only pleasure that he records with his calamus (a bamboo reed used for a pen, with ochre or carbon black powder, wetted down from its stick-form to ink) was his arrival. He always got a particular pleasure from admiring his handsomely decorated metal pen-box, which most likely came from Persia. Ibn Battuta was no naturalist by inclination, and would not have been pleased at all to have been lucky enough to have seen that largest of all brids, the ostrich, on his desert voyage (Leo Africanus listed animals in his notebook). It had taken him two very long months to reach Walata, and the sun seemed to have concentrated itself right in the center of his forehead. The only possible empathy he could feel, probably, by this time was with the lowly toad of the desert who hides under a stone until the night falls and shuts out the sun.

At Walata he had sent a messenger to inform the Emperor of Mali of his arrival. It cannot be accurately said that he was in the best of temper when taking the place assigned by protocol for him to meet the Emperor's representative. His mind was dwelling on a most interesting feature of his journey. His caravan had been lost for some days, and had been led back to its route by a blind guide. It seems that this guide used his sense of smell, "by the smell (he writes) he declared the situation of the place." Thinking of this at the time, his attention could not have been fully fixed on the important emissary sent by the Emperor. Alas! the meeting was distasteful to him, in fact he found the man insolent, and could not help regretting that he had ever started the journey.

A stay of fifty days in Walata seemed to sweeten his temper and to gladden his eye. His comments on the beauty of the women are profuse; but he thought (cutting off the end of his pen to sharpen it) the women were allowed too much freedom!

His trip to Niani included only a few guides. On his way he mistakenly called the Niger River the Nile, whose source and destination was not determined for centuries after. The roads were safe, and so he had no need of the extra protection he felt he must have at the outset, when a much larger party accompanied him. He carried with him beads, spices and salt, so that he could buy food. He lauded the safety of the roads later on, and found no trouble in getting sufficient food. Barter was the only means of exchange in the small villages, in larger cities gold was used. It is a little known fact that actual banking facilities were highly developed in the Middle Ages in the Moslem world. One time in the course of his world travels, Ibn Battuta actually successfully concluded a transaction that had his money sent from India to Morocco.

In Niani he found the customs similar to those of the king of Ghana, full of opulence, and beautifully staged. He could not approve of the sprinkling of dust on the heads; an act of obeisance to the king. Leo Africanus two centuries later could not abide this custom either: he said, "Those that speak to him (the king) must fall down before his feet, and must sprinkle their heads with earth. This was the protocol for those who have never had an audience—such as an ambassador or a prince." Ibn Battuta's sharp eye did note at the time of his presentation at court that there were two goats present for protection against the evil eye—This was Mansa Sulayman's court.

His first impression of the great Mansa Musa's brother was not at all favorable . . . "He is a miserly king, not a man from whom one might hope a rich present." This did not at all dampen his enthusiasm in his description of the king. He wore a velvety red tunic, he said rhapsodically, preceeded by musicians carrying gold and silver guitars, following behind him were 300 armed slaves. The king moved in a very leisurely fashion, affecting a slow movement, and stopped with great dramatic effect from time to time.

There is every indication that Ibn Battuta's temper improved with time. He stayed eight months and found the king more generous than his first quick judgment implied. His mood seemed improved considerably when he was given free board and lodgings for his lengthy stay. It is very likely that Ibn Battuta's annoyance initially stemmed from the fact that he was not treated by his host with the customary reverence that is accorded to Arabic scholars almost automatically. Pious Moslems look upon Arabic writing as sacred, because the Koran is written in that language. Most of the time these illiterate peoples extend the reverence for the writing to the scholar, he is regarded as a holy man by many.

His observations of the workings of the Empire were seriously noted down at length. "The Negroes," he said, "possess some admirable qualities. They are seldom unjust, and have a great abhorrence of injustice than any other people." He cites an example of this exemplary behavior: There was actually a complaint made against the governor of Walata (governed as a province). The governor who had paid tribute to the Emperor was accused of some financial irregularity, it is not completely clear just what it was. In any case he was brought to Niani almost immediately, and found guilty and punished, and the man who lodged the complaint against him received his money back.

As to the individual's relation to the Emperor, he wrote, "they did not confiscate the property of any white man who dies in their country, even if it be uncounted wealth. On the contrary, they give it into the charge of some trustworthy person among the white, until the rightful heir takes possession of it."

Although he was traveling in behalf of the Sultan of Fez, he could not afford a horse, so he left Niani by camel, noting a visit to Timbuktu, at which he stopped. He wrote that he passed the tomb of Es-Saheli the architect-poet. Leo Africanus claimed several centuries later that over the mosque that Es-Saheli designed, there was a half legible inscription over the principle gate. It says "un excellente maestro de Granada." Ibn Battuta exchanged, as planned, salt and spices for butter and meat, and he resumed his travels by canoe; he noted in a general observation that the inhabitants lived in "luxury and ease." It is here that Ibn Battuta's penned notes of his travels end, for he was summoned home to Fez.

Following Mansa Sulayman's death in 1359, rivalry broke out, and the country was beset by civil strife. Kamba, Mansa Sulayman's son was felled in such a conquest for power.

A new ruler finally emerged calling himself Mari Jata II; in an effort to further pursue good relations with Fez, which had lapsed during the palace quarrels, Mari Jata sent a giraffe to the Sultan as a gift. This gift made the impression that was wanted—it caused a sensation!

From here on we must follow the winding course of the Mandingo history from grandeur to dissolution with the help of Ibn Khaldun, a contemporary of Ibn Battuta, and a literary man of distinction. Ibn Khaldun had a taste for court intrigue which caused his imprisonment by Abu Inan in Fez. This did not diminish his position in the community as a scholar, as he had occupied many responsible positions in the community at the behest of his royal patron. After his imprisonment in 1357 he returned to Tunis, anxious to resume his monumental work on the "History of the Berbers." Around this period he again was tantalized into court intrigues, and suddenly found it expedient to make a sudden pilgrimage to Mecca. Arriving in Cairo he found that his scholarly reputation had preceeded him and that people were clamouring for instruction, so he stayed on.

It was during his Egyptian stay and in the course of his studies and research that he acquired valuable information on the early kings of Mali from Shaykh 'Uthman, faqih ahl Ghana, a famous Moslem jurist, known for his erudition and piety. One such ruler of Mali, at one time he learned, left his country to discover for himself the limits of the ocean. The events recorded by Ibn Khaldun take in a period of 30 years of the Mali Empire, the only source for this information, unless the findings of archeologists will in the future provide additional knowledge. His pen sketches a picture of a troubled state, this he learned from no less than the Mali Ambassador to Egypt, who was present at the time. From a Moslem judge, who had settled in Gao, but who came from Sijilmasa he gained considerable information, for that was the starting or culminating point for the caravans. It was apparently from this man that he learned, that the famous gold nugget of Ghana was sold to some Egyptian merchants for lack of money in order to offset the extravagances of the Emperor. Mari Jata died of sleeping sickness in 1374 and was succeeded by his son Musa II. An energetic person, he sought to rebuild the Empire that was almost in ruins due to Mari Jata's extensive and personal liquidation of the treasury.

The campaigns of Musa II led him beyond Gao and to a military confrontation with Omar ben Idris, the Sultan of Bornu, a formidable adversary. Bornu enters the stream of knowable history in the 8th century, with a dynasty first established in Kanem (Northern Nigeria). This dynasty held sway until 1846, which is said to be the longest dynastic reign recorded anywhere in the world.

A deflation of the power of Mali is clearly indicated in the 15th century. Although in decay, its territory was still considerable. It is not clear whether Mali ever exercised any influence on the historically elusive Tekrur.

Ibn Khaldun's history closes in 1390 after the succession of Maghan III. The recorded history of this extensive land of the Negroes rests at that point.

In 1962 experts seeking the site of the ancient Mali flew over what was Niani and reported that there was nothing visible from the air at the confluence of the Niger and Sankarem. Upon closer inspection on the ground, at Niani, some heaps of clay were found.

Here lie the remnants of a great Empire in the form of broken bits of clay. With the emergence of the 20th century state of Mali, a new impetus for the investigation of her past has been provided.

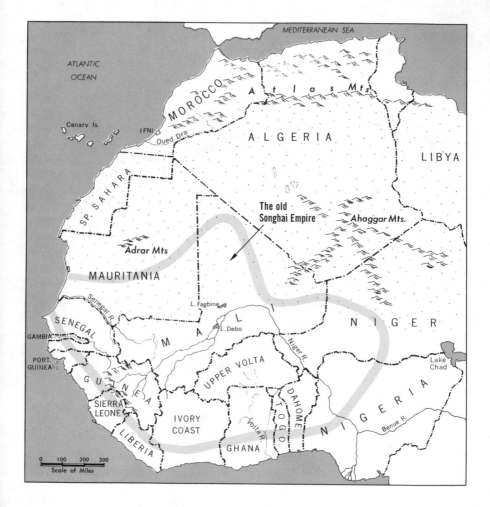

The old
Songhai Empire

IV

African Empires—Songhai

Mali, whose Empire covered a wide circle, with the Niger bend as its center, did not break up as the influence of the Songhai began to spread . . . it gradually dispersed. Interestingly enough, the Songhai managed to become the greatest Empire in the Western Sudan, but they never were more than a minority of the total population.

The Songhai entered history as a people in 700 A.D. They were originally ruled by a dynasty of Berbers who had been swept out of Tripolitania (Libya) by the first Arab conquest. The traditional home of the Songhai was Dendi, not far above the Busa Rapids of Nigeria, where centuries later the Scottish explorer Mungo Park was claimed by the river. Their ancient capital, called Kukia, though not in existence today, was southeast of Gao on the right bank of the Niger River. It was in this approximate area that the Songhai settled, and from there administered their vast lands. The Songhai, or at least their kings, had been Moslems since 1009, fifty years before the Almoravids.

At the beginning of the 14th century, it may be recalled, Mansa Musa tried to weaken his growing contender for power by holding hostage the two sons of his Songhai rival. Both escaped, but it was Ali Kolen, after his return to Gao, who promptly ascended the throne and declared his independence from the Mandingos of the already waning Mali Empire. Ali Kolen chose for himself the title of Sonni. He was succeeded by his brother Sonni Sulayman Nar, and in the following century, though we have no certain knowledge of the occurrences of this time, we do know that the Songhai were ruled by 16 successive descendants of Ali Kolen. Although the Songhai of Gao retained their independence for a century after their liberation from the Mandingos of Mali, Mali was not so weak as to allow the descendants of Ali Kolen to live in peace. Assaults were made again and again upon the Songhai, but the Mandingos of Mali had lost their initial cohesiveness and could not gain a victory.

In 1433, Akil ag Malway, chief of the Maghcharen, a Tuareg tribe, subdued all remaining resistance and ruled the city of Gao for 35 years. Basically a nomad, who had to adjust to town life, Akil felt confined, and entrusted the government of this once great city to a Sanhaja from Adraa, one Muhammad Naddiwo, a man who had previously held this post under the Mali Empire. Muhammad Naddiwo was succeeded by his son Omar, who not long thereafter got into a dispute with his overlord Akil. The collection of taxes and tributes was at the heart of the trouble. Omar, a governor, under the prevailing system of the Empire was entitled to a third of the taxes, two thirds to be spread about among his supporters. Akil had never been satisfied with this arrangement, and when Muhammad Naddi, Omar's father, died, Akil took to raiding the city of Timbuktu around tax collection time. Not only did he do this, but he took to brutally disrupting the life of the city by attacking the women, and raiding the houses of ordinary citizens. Omar by this time, was desperate, he felt that the only person that he could effectively turn to, was the king of the Songhai, at that time Sonni Ali.

Sonni Ali was quick to answer this plea for help, seeing all its possibilities, and thought that it was worth his personal intervention. Sonni Ali's help did not bode well for Timbuktu. Leading his cavalry, he marched up to the bank of the Niger, keeping as he did the river between himself and the Tuareg nomads, who had not yet occupied the country on the south. He appeared to Akil and Omar such a fearsome and fordmidable sight, as he reached a point nearly opposite Timbuktu, that, they immediately fled to Walata in the desert. A general wave of fear seemed also to have been experienced by the literary men of Sankore University, and many distinguished scholars exited also. Omar, who had been more than toying with the idea of a reward for calling in Sonni Ali, fled too.

Sonni Ali captured Timbuktu at about 1468, he came not bearing kindness for these Berbers of Timbuktu, but bearing the sword. The Songhai people, of which Sonni Ali was the most prominent, were of Berber descent, a people who had intermingled with the Negroes. This did not deter Sonni Ali from slaying the learned and the pious of Timbuktu, and putting to death the Berbers who had always pretended that they were culturally superior to the Songhai. Es-Sadi, the great historian of Timbuktu recalled that the Islamic creed had no real depth in the heart of Sonni Ali, and did not hesitate to revile him. "Only God knows (he said) how many people he killed." He vented his wrath in his writings, a now famous collection of documents in Arabic called the *Tarikh es Soudan*. Libertine, tyrant, scoundrel, no description was hateful enough. This ruthlessness was rationalized by Sonni Ali on the grounds that the inhabitants of Timbuktu were in an alliance with the Tuareg, the hereditary enemies of the Songhai. Es-Sadi objectively informs us that this destruction continued for two years.

Sonni Ali's energy could not be quenched. Always seeking new outlets, he now turned his attention to the rivulets and swamps of the Niger, and eyed the city of Jenne jealously. This city still exists, approximately 250 miles from Timbuktu. Jenne had always been defended by nature. Secure for 800 years, she was protected by the rise and fall of the waters of this network of waterways by which she was so happily surrounded. A "blessed town" is how it was described, a market center for salt from Taghaza and gold from Bitu (Bonduku), it too like Timbuktu attracted and acquired cultured residents in the active pursuit of learning. Here on this northern littoral the roots of culture could be planted with more confidence. Spared the interruption of invaders as Timbuktu had to face, little uprooting had taken place. Leo Africanus gave this same impression of Jenne, he described how the "priests and doctors of their law go apparelled in white cotton, the rest of the inhabitants being clad in black or blue cloth."

It took years for Sonni Ali to capture Jenne, he was spurred on by the knowledge that learned men like Es-Sadi, a bitter denouncer of him later, prized this city too.

The waters surrounding this city did what they had always done, and will do, they rose and formed a watery barricade to the forces of Sonni Ali. Not to be outdone by nature, the great Songhai, Sonni Ali was prepared to wait. As he waited, famine overtook his troops, it was terrible, Sonni Ali exhausted, with the morale of his men very low, was just about to call off the siege when the city surrendered. Jenne was his in 1473. The city apparently escaped the ravages of Timbuktu, for the reason that they had held out no hand of friendship to the Tuaregs.

Determined and made bold by this success, he felt that his ambitions were yet to be fully realized. Not long after his marriage to the queen mother of Jenne, he launched a series of campaigns against small kingdoms; he raided the Fulani, and harried the peoples west of Lake Debo. Setting out further south and west, he met setbacks, and his advances were stemmed.

He returned to Gao about three years after the capture of that great jewel in his crown, Jenne. He had always had a particular talent for keenly smarting over his losses; he still resented the fact that the literati of Timbuktu had escaped to Walata, in what seemed to him to be a hastily contrived exit.

Walata experienced no peace during this period, the Mossi of Yatenga, daringly in 1480 attacked Walata. The Mossi, an offshoot of the Mandingos, are a great block of Negro peoples coming from the interior watershed of the Volta River (the state of Upper Volta today). Although they raided and fought their influential and powerful neighbors of the Niger, they had never been subjugated or ruled by outsiders. Islam had almost no effect on the over two million people of this group. It is thought that the Mossi, then as today, making an intellectual exception by erasing the marks of French colonization, must be very much like the Mandingo peoples before they launched out on a career of empire building, and before the incursion of Islam.

Around this period, Omar, the former governor of Timbuktu, who had capitulated so instantaneously at the sight of Sonni Ali's forces, suddenly re-emerged, organized a pursuit and recovered many of the captives that had been carried off at the sacking of Timbuktu. Such were the loyalties to this great city!

There is no doubt that Sonni Ali was an enterprising man with an imagination of no little scope. Not long after the Mossi attacked Walata, he reestablished his headquarters at the western tip of Lake Fagbine, and there he conceived a fastastic plan to add Walata to the Empire. So anxious was he to add Walata to a formidable list of conquests, that he conceived of building a canal from Lake Fagbine to Walata. Taking into consideration minor geographic changes, it is said that Lake Fagbine might have extended further west than it does today, and that the canal would have to have been about 200 miles long. While Sonni Ali was trying to implement this plan, the Mossi were continuing to threaten him, and before he could carry it out, he had to divert his considerable energies in 1483 to repel the Mossi. The Mossi were being guided and encouraged by a new leader, one Nassare. Subsequently, the Mossi were defeated and pushed back to their country of Yatenga. The Mossi leader found the Songhis still a very formidable foe, and after having been defeated by them, took out their frustration on the Mandingos of Mali, who by that time were being terribly pressed by the Songhai in the north and the Fulani of Futa (Guinea) in the west. The Mandingos of the once great Mali Empire, much diminished by this time, in desperation called upon the Portuguese for aid. The Portuguese already had trading posts along the West Coast of Africa, the fruits of Prince Henry's (the navigator) efforts, and they turned a deaf ear to the Mandingos. The Portuguese who had been given trading posts by Sonni Ali would hardly be expected to come to the aid of a much diminished rival.

Not content to let the scholars of Timbuktu in peace, Sonni Ali continued to hound them, eventually they fled to Aukar—and how they prayed for his death. In 1492, when Columbus was setting sail for America, their prayers were answered, and after a reign of 26 years Sonni Ali was inundated by natural forces; he drowned in a river in the course of a raid. There was no doubt that Sonni Ali had immense energy and a talent for the winning of battles. His son and heir to the throne did not prove so adept.

From the moment that his son (Bakari Da'a) took the throne, he was confronted with a rival Muhammad Ture, a Negro Soninke. He fought and lost a battle with his rival at Angoo, near Gao. Thus fell the ancient Lemta dynasty, rulers of the Songhai for 8 centuries.

If the candle of culture had been extinguished by Sonni Ali, it was to be relit under this new monarch Muhammad Ture, who assumed the title of Askia Muhammad I. If the mantle of learning was now to be worn proudly, so would the rites of religion be more deeply respected in the person of this new king.

Askia I had one great strength, which could be observed from the outset, he did not consider it a weakness to ask the advice of those better educated than himself. It was in this manner that the cultured of Timbuktu regained stature. This more enlightened atmosphere brought back the exiles from Walata to Gao and they rejoiced in their new found appreciation. Askia from the first showed a genius for political organization. He had been a General and a Prime Minister under Sonni Ali, and knew the needs of the country. As Islam revived so also trade was stimulated, and Gao and Timbuktu experienced a new prosperity.

Many important developments took place during the reign of Askia, when Songhai was soaring to new heights as an Empire. Askia the Great as Muhammad I came to be called, conducted his campaigns in the spirit of the Hadj, and his successes were being noticed by the Western world. Islam flowered under Askia, as surely as the Niger flowed downstream. In this surge of a newly revived religious force, a twig was yet to fall and to lodge in this stream. This twig which fell so imperceptibly into the stream of a Moslem revival brought with it to Gao one Muhammad Abd el Kerim el Maghili. He was one of those stringent apostles of Islam. A citizen of Tlemcen (Algeria), his fervour had carried him from his home to Tuat miles away. He preached to the very exclusion of the Jews of Tuat, and in fact it was his preaching that initiated their destruction. The rest of the citizens of Tuat, who were the very target of El Baghadadi, as he was called, found him too austere to contain in their midst, and so they forced him to flee. It was just such a flight that took him to other communities like Katsina and Kano, which actually had the effect of enlivening his reputation as a reformer and religious leader. One day as he was traveling in the direction of the Songhai capital, Gao, he received a message—that the few Jews left in Tuat had flown in the face of their commandants, they had killed his son in revenge. He arrived in Gao dispirited and exhausted. Amid the splendor of the court of Askia we find him pleading with this Emperor to kill the Jews of Gao, it is clear that Askia was sympathetic, but could not comply with such a request. Aside from the tragedy that followed this fervid reformer of Islam, it is clear that Askia found him most wise in other things and in fact invited him to stay. During his stay, Askia put to this North African theologian questions concerning the behavior of his people. He sought answers, from this man, who he knew to be educated, because he was seeking a program of social reform, he was anxious that his people should act rightly, and that these "rules" should be codified. Ali Maghili's replies are said to be still well known among the Moslems of West Africa. There was no doubt that this man advised Askia wisely on the day to day problems of administration of the Empire, and from all accounts he was a very successful counselor.

The political organization of Askia I stretched through the Western Sudan, and much of what he did was tempered by great wisdom. Along with the formation of a standing army, he was keenly aware that one could not bring unwilling peoples into one's kingdom with the use of military force alone. So, henceforward he partitioned the kingdom, clipping out provinces and providing Governors who served as chief executives over assigned areas. Many times, the small kingdoms that were conquered were shorn of their kings, and replaced with Governors. Timbuktu and Jenne had Mayors, or their equivalent. He appointed a high Admiral from the Sorko, a traditional fishing people, and he picked a high priest to look after the needs of the pagans and non-Moslems. Actually the authority was shared among Ministers and dignitaries. The kingship was run as a kind of parliamentary affair.

The ascendance to the throne was no disorganized affair. A king could not be designated unless electors approved first; they were usually part of the royal family. The royal duties could not be fulfilled unless the king had been enthroned according to certain consecrating rites. In fact, a king could be unmade under this system. A king made by conquests, as many were, was by no means in total possession of the ground of his own kingdom. He had power, true, over the life and death of the hapless inhabitants, but he was restrained on the question of land. Decisions to be made on the ownership of land were passed upon by the patriarch of the group, even if he was the humblest man in the kingdom. There was usually a non-partial person who was delegated as "master of the ground" or "chief of the land . . ." It is in this spirit of accommodation to all different peoples that this vast Empire was organized, with checks and balances of its own.

His mind, active, and fired by his religious beliefs, led him to make a pilgrimage to Mecca, scaled every bit as much to the proportions of Mansa Musa's memorable trek a century and a half before. His first thought was to carry with him gold for distribution to the various charities in the holy cities. He set aside 300,000 gold pieces from the treasury, one-third of which would go to charity. In his caravan, he was accompanied by 500 cavalrymen and 1,000 foot soldiers. Interestingly enough, this caravan, which was every bit as lustrous as Mansa Musa's, whose person and pilgrimage had excited so much comment, appears to have been little noticed, because of this great man's modesty.

Returning from his pilgrimage, refreshed and reaffirmed in his faith, he decided in 1497 to return to Gao. This pilgrimage was very costly and exceeded the 300,000 gold pieces that he carried with him. Now he was determined to extend his Empire, and all his campaigns were carried out with the added inspiration provided by the Hadj. It was in this spirit that he led a jihad against the Mossi. Although his army carried off many slaves, they still retained their independence. Then his thoughts turned west, he felt that he must extinguish Mali once and for all, Mali, dimmed as she was as an Empire, capitulated, too weak to resist.

Askia and his efforts towards unification had its difficulties, one of which was that he could not be absolutely sure of the loyalty of his troops. It was most unsettling, but a logical outcome of trying to encompass so many diverse groups. In certain battles his troops showed too much affinity with the foe. Just three years after his victorious bout with the remnants of the Mali Empire, he set out from Gao, and attacked Borgu downstream along the Niger at Say. Askia had heavy losses there, but no great regrets, as many of his casualities were relatives of the people of the area. His western border was advanced right up to the borders of Tekrur, near Senegal. Rumors extended the Empire at one time from Taghaza in the desert to the Ocean.

It was the various peoples of the Hausa states, whose population were Negro, but who also boasted of a strong strain of Berber in them, that were of great importance to the Emperor. They were Gobir, Kano, Zaria, Katsina, and their importance was known enough to attract the Barbary merchants. They were farmers, weavers, smiths, and leather workers. These states ran eastward from the Niger in the direction of Lake Chad. They were well watered and generally fertile regions. In traveling today through Zaria to Kano, which offered stiff resistance to the invaders of that time, one is keenly conscious of their independence and individuality, which in the early 1500's were their handicaps. Then they were too individualistic to unite for war, being a peaceful people, and hence they were an easy prey to invaders, lacking as they did, any natural defenses, like fortifications.

The victory over the Islamic Hausa states brought with it outright conflict with their hereditary enemies, the Tuareg. The Tuaregs mercilessly raided the Hausas, as had their Tuareg brothers, who had menaced the Niger villages. Askia's eastern campaigns included Air, which he knew to be the haven of the Tuaregs; however, he was far too clever to spend his energy in pursuing them to their desert stronghold; he was content to drive them out into the surrounding desert. The French in the 20th century had a similar problem with the Tuaregs, and they found that the most hurtful insurance against their incursions, at which they were expert, was to deprive

them of their grazing grounds.

Askia, at this time, had as an ally and companion in arms, one Kanta, King of Kebbi, which was a small vassal state, who no doubt paid tribute to him. It was located between Hausa and the Niger. A combatant and ally in the eastern campaigns of Askia, Kanta became dissatisfied with the parsimonious way in which he was regarded for his friendship. He rebelled quite suddenly against Askia, and apparently, with all his wits about him, declared Kebbi independent. He had thought it all through quite clearly, and this was a move predicated on his intimate knowledge of the Songhai army, and more important on its weaknesses. He felt that his little state had a strategic advantage, as it was located in the marshes, which were found to be unconquerable. His calculated risk took into account two important factors: one, that his people were supporting him; two, that his seven stone walls, called the walls of Surame would hold off an enemy effectively. The ruins still stand today. Askia was defeated at these walls. The people of Kebbi, the Kebbawa, not only defied their powerful overlord, the Songhai, but those seven walls held back invaders from Bornu, once a powerful kingdom east of Lake Chad.

When the British conquered Sokoto, they found that a descendant of Kebbi had been holding out against these same kinds of incursions, and that the legend of Kanta's canoe, which is said to still lie in the marshes, still lived.

Askia's energy and drive expanded a great Empire, and its people lived in relative security within its borders. His great achievements were only to be unbalanced by family disturbances. It was during this time, that his sons rebelled. Old and quite tired from his imperial gains, going blind, and exhausted from the task of administering such a far-flung Empire, he called upon his brother Yahia to help him. He could not reason with his sons, even with the intervention of his brother. All hope lost of bringing his truculent sons into line, violence broke out, and Yahia died pleading with his nephews for family tranquility. In 1528, Musa, a son of Askia, humiliatingly forced the elderly monarch to abdicate. And so the man Askia the Great, who brought with his reign peace and prospertiy, organized within the framework of a well-run government,

was pushed aside.

Mansa, who exiled his aging father to a desolate island, was so tyrannical, that his people could only endure him for three years; they finally assassinated him. He was succeeded by Askia Bengan Korei, who sent an expedition against Kanta, and as the leader, was humiliatingly defeated. No one ever tried to conquer the Kebbi again. Ismail, his brother, followed him to the throne. It was about this time that Askia the Great died, a very unhappy man. Askia Ishak succeeded Ismail. He carried out several campaigns, one against Dendi, and the other an attack on the Mandingo capital, but never occupied it. Ishak enhanced the prestige of the Empire and was forthright in his handling of the affairs of state.

About three years after Ishak took the throne, the Sultan of Morocco, Muhammad ech-Cheikh, conceived of the idea of controlling the Sudanese trade. His idea was to gain the salt mines of Taghaza, whose produce was the means of exchange for gold, his final object. Without hesitation, and with a high degree of confidence, he sent a note to Askia Ishak, asking him to cede these mines to him immediately. His answer to the Moroccan Sultan's request came in the form of 2,000 Tuaregs, who carried out a raid on Dra'a, south of Morocco; these troops were careful not to kill anyone. Three years later Ishak died. Daud succeeded his brother, and he too had his quarrels with the Kebbi. He was the first, however, to conclude a peace treaty with these plucky people, the first of its kind in the area.

Daud, so recorded Es-Sadi, launched a raid of 24 horsemen against the Hausa city of Katsina. He relates the shocking story of how the Songhai horsemen literally threw themselves at a body of 400 Katsina men killing up to 15, wounding about 9 and including in the toll a high official. The Katsinawa were enraged at this attack which they beat off with their superior forces, but they could not help but admire such headstrong bravery. As a result of this, they sent back the many captives they had taken, with word that such brave men did not deserve to die.

Although the regime of Ishak first made contact, which emerged into conflict with the Moroccans, Daud,

too was experiencing a renewal of Moroccan interest in the Sudan. Mulay Ahmed El-Mansur in 1578, who succeeded his father as Sultan, tried to lease the mines from Daud. His father, in the days of his reign carried out a raid on Taghaza, and killed the Songhai governor. Raids on the precious salt mines caused the Songhai, who refused to work the mines for the Moroccans, to dig another mine at Taodeni as an alternate source for salt, which still is in use today.

Coexistence was restored between the Sudan and Morocco briefly with the arrival of an ambassador from the Sultan with a gift of 10,000 pieces of gold; this civility was meant to keep the trade flowing between the two areas. The Moroccans never let "desert politics" interfere with the free flow of trade.

The Songhai Empire was now trading with the Maghreb (or the West), as Barbary came to be called by the Arabs, on a scale that exceeded the hope of Mansa Musa and the Mandingos of Mali. The vast lands of the Songhai now stretched from the rain forests, north to the Sahara, east to Hausa, and to the Atlantic in the west. A multiplicity of skills was encompassed within the Empire, practiced by a hard working people who ate well, and lacked nothing. In fact they had a surplus of slaves and gold, which is what stimulated the Moroccan interest in them.

Following the death of Daud in 1582, and during the reign of his son, Muhammad El Hadj, an unexpected visitor came to Gao bearing gifts from the Moroccan Sultan, now El-Mansur. It was later learned that this guest was making a military reconnaissance of the area, for not long after his visit, the Moroccans sent an army with the object of attacking Timbuktu. Es-Sadi's report, unconfirmed by any other source, says that they perished in the Mauritanian desert from thirst. El-Ufrani, a Moorish historian, is strangely silent in his works about this incident.

The Moors of Morocco, under El-Mansur, were determined to invade the Sudan, for the Sultan had long become hypnotized by this idea, even when it had been called fantastic by many of his close associates. It was the source of the gold trade, that he must have; and to attack it meant a 1500 mile march across the desert,

which had never been attempted. He was well aware that whole armies could perish in the open desert.

It was under the leadership of a blue-eyed Spaniard from Las Cuevas, in Granada, called Judar, that 4,000 men, and 9,000 transport animals set out for their invasion. Although the number of transport animals seems excessive for 4,000 men, it was not. There would be times during this 1500 mile trek across that sea of sand, where they would be completely dependent upon their own supplies. Judar led his troops from Marrakech on October 1590, and took a route south over the Atlas mountains into the province of Dra'a. He could hardly keep such a huge force a secret, since he had to travel along a popular trade route, with a certainty of finding oases.

It took 20 weeks to reach the Niger. There are no descriptions of this journey, or how many men and beasts perished during this grueling march, but losses must have been considerable. It was a splendid army, picked for its hardiness, and they were in battle readiness to the extent that they carried with them 31,000 pounds of gun powder, a similar weight in lead, morions, shot, tow, pitch, resin, ropes, spades, and the like.

Askia Ishak II was taken completely by surprise by the invasion of the Moors. Although he was aware of how perfidious they could be, both he and his people could not believe that any group of men would have the fortitude to launch an invasion from 1500 miles away—across a desert. His people did not respond to his call to arms, and the Songhai troops were badly beaten at Tondibi, about 35 miles from Gao. Judar was more frustrated than dazzled when he entered Gao, the townspeople had fled with all the gold available. The Emperor Askia Ishak II, saw no other course than to negotiate with the enemy, and made the important concession to the Moors, that of the right to import salt from the Sudan.

Judar's army was falling apart from exhaustion and disease, and he himself was not feeling rewarded by the capture of Gao since no vast treasury of gold had been found . . . he knew that the Sultan would be far from satisfied. El-Mansur did not believe Judar that there was no gold to be found there, and so he replaced this commander with one Mahmud ben-Zegun, who he thought could wrest the gold from the intractable Sudanese. Muhmud Pasha as he was called, shifted the strategy of the campaign, and routed the Songhai army by pursuing them downstream by boat, they had been fighting solely a land battle previously. The Songhai, in the depths of the misery of military defeat, produced a great and capable leader called Askia Nuh, who rallied the forces of the Songhai brilliantly. Askia Nuh held out for years against superior forces, and more effective weapons. The Moroccan commander, by this time, was beginning to see a certain futility in the entire struggle, but he was a tenacious man. El-Mansur received a note from him explaining the woeful condition of his troops, and asking for reinforcements, he got these along with a message expressing increased respect for his commander.

The Moorish invasion caused the Songhai Empire to fragment, and the cohesiveness, that was the hallmark of its accomplishment, broke up into warring tribes, encouraging pillage and anarchy. Jenne was ravaged, the peoples of the lake region above Timbuktu were attacked, and the Tuareg took advantage of the peoples who had already been weakened by the raids of others. About this time Timbuktu rose up against the Moors stationed there, but Mahmud had been clever and had sent Mami ben-Barun back there to hold the city. Apparently Mami was the only Moor who showed any sympathy with the Negroes, he even went as far as to apologize for the excesses of the troops. Mami attempted to subdue the Tuareg, who had fallen upon Timbuktu in great number. His success against these wily fighters was due to new replacements sent from Morocco, already strained by the Sudanese adventure.

Mahmud, unlike Mami, felt no compassion for the people. He tricked the people of Timbuktu cruelly and squeezed their valuables from them. The people of Timbuktu suffered terribly under the Moors, imprisoned and robbed they withstood unbearable cruelties. El-Mansur, not deaf to the word that he received from the middle Niger was angered by these abuses of Mahmud Pasha; he summarily dispatched a man to take over and put him to death. Mahmud received word from a friend of the fate that was to befall him. This was during the time he was trying to dislodge Askia Nuh from hiding. He launched a reckless campaign which was to be his last for he had planned to escape after a victory. He was killed during this poorly planned skirmish. Nuh died in battle not long thereafter and so the resistance of the Songhai collapsed. The Songhai were far from broken in spirit by the Moors. Enfeebled by four years of battle, the Moors were by no means in control of the Empire.

The influence of the Moors on the middle Niger caused untold suffering to the peoples of the Western Sudan, who were confronted by them. A peaceful people, they resisted as best they could, but the superior fire-power of the Moroccans overcame them. The Moors did have cultural influence on the Western Sudan, in the architecture, dress and diet, especially in Jenne. Es-Sadi says that when Spanish had all but been forgotten the people could still recall with horror the Spanish order "cut off his head."

V
Two Highways

Two highways have played vital parts as passageways in the history of the Western Sudan. One is the Niger, the world's tenth largest river. The other is the Sahara, the largest continuous desert on the earth's surface. Both have been causeways for commerce and thoroughfares down which thought, too, has traveled.

The middle Niger, arid about its banks, until it dips to Jenne, is handicapped through want of boat building materials. Had this material, the fan palm, been available in quantity, this water-course would have had accelerated traffic, like that of the desert routes. If more boats had been available along the Niger River, the stream of political events might have significantly shifted.

The introduction of the camel to the Sahara revolutionized the trans-Sahara crossings. Human beings have been criss-crossing the Sahara from time immemorial. Trails that pass over the *hammada,* the bedrock, have been so polished in certain areas as to indicate that the bare feet of numberless human porters passed that way.

It is not clear whether the Romans were responsible for the introduction of this valuable beast with the remarkable metabolism to Africa. Camels were first heard of in 46 B.C. at the battle of Thepsus, when included in the booty that Caesar captured from Juba were some 22 camels. In 363 A.D., Romanus is said to have demanded 4,000 camels from Leptis Magna for his army. He would have had occasion to own camels, being so close to the Libyan desert. The transportation difficulties that the Romans had in their administration were immense, and it is not at all improbable that they thought that the importation of camels from Asia would accelerate trade.

The Sahara, by its nature, is sparsely populated. What is remarkable about this barren expanse of sand and stone, almost as large as the United States, is, that it has supported and spawned some distinctive human groupings like that of the Berber dynasties, who, because they had ingeniously adapted, survived, and still cling in some groups to their ancient and disciplined nomadic way of life. The Berbers, were just as important a spur to the growth of the West African medieval empires as was the Sahara; a vast and sandy highway, across which cultures were diffused and trade expanded.

In part, the history of the medieval Western Sudan is one of the conquest of small farmers or tillers of the soil by well organized and predatory Tuaregs; it was through the Berber Tuaregs that Islam penetrated to the southern fringe of the Sahara. The foremost example is the thrust, south of the Sahara, made by the Almoravids, leading to the capture of Ghana and its conversion to Islam. Following this successful incursion of Islam into the Ghana Empire, it picked up momentum in the succeeding empires of Mali and Songhai. Because of this significant spread of Islam through this area, Professor George Murdock says, in *Africa, Its Peoples and Their Culture History*, that the southern fringe of the Sahara constitutes "the African frontier of the Moslem world and of the great Middle Eastern culture area." Others, like E.W. Bovill, in *Caravans of the Old Sahara*, feel strongly that the conquests made in the Western Sudan by the shepherd kings (the various Berber tribes), "put iron into the blood of the conquered, but in so doing absorb their superior culture. It was to such unions that the Western Sudanese owe their gift for political organization which enabled them more than once to achieve imperial greatness." Professor Melville Hershkovits, an Africanist and anthropologist throws a different light on the matter in, *The Human Factor in Changing Africa*, he says, "Certainly it is difficult to sustain the proposition that Africans learned of the territorial state from invaders to the north, particularly in view of the extent to which the forms of this institution were developed in the more southerly coastal forested belt." The Mossi states to the south, to cite one example, are not included in the ancient Sudanese Empires. They were sheltered from all foreign influence, or non-Negro influences, and maintained their own political institutions which are indigenous in origin.

The tracing of the Sahara by well traveled caravan routes brought Islam in its train, and the arts and acts of its civilization; along with its many levels of cultural encrustation. Africa had always been thought to be a continent that "derived" its civilization from elsewhere. It was traditionally thought that black Africa had always been a recipient, and never a donor, to the life-history of man.

Long before the caravans from the north sought systematically and coveteously the gold, ivory and slaves from the little known interior, Africa had made her contribution; our failure to recognize it, is one of the most tragic distortions of world history.

It is generally acknowledged that the shift of a civilization, from food-gathering to the actual cultivation of domestic plants, represents progress. This happened in the Neolithic age in Egypt and in the Western Sudan at the same time . . . but independently. Ancient Egypt acquired domestic animals and agriculture from southwest Asia. Iraqi village life had shifted in 6500 B.C. from the sedentary, to tilling, along with the keeping of goats, and this diffused throughout the Fertile Crescent. These achievements reached lower Egypt about 4500 B.C., we learn this from the method of radiocarbon dating. This became the base after more than a millenium for the splendid civilization of Pharaonic Egypt.

What is little known, is that the Negro in the western part of Africa was developing agriculture at the same time and independently, not borrowing from other peoples, but inventing it on his own. Professor George Murdock explains that this far-reaching error is due to the botanist Vavilov. He says that this came about because Vavilov, who had added the most to our knowledge of the origins of cultivated plants, had personally investigated every major and minor center of independent domestication in the world, but never visited black Africa. His error was, says Professor Murdock, in ascribing some important strains to lesser Ethiopia and India. As time went on, the mistake compounded itself. The plants in question had spread before the dawn of the Christian era to India, and when the Europeans came upon them, they assumed that they were of local origin. Botanists are frequently helpful in the field of historical reconstruction. They find that the place of origin of a plant can be found by locating the native habitat of its wild form. Plants, even if crossed, retain their separate identities due to their genetic structure. Negro Africa, says Professor Murdock, ranks as "one of the four major agricultural complexes evolved in the entire course of history—we must now align the West African Negroes as one of mankind's leading creative benefactors."

Other confirmation comes from what anthropologists calls liguistic distributions. It is expected that a people, who have progressed from hunting to food-gathering on an organized agricultural basis, naturally multiply and expand at the expense of their more backward neighbors. The result would be that their language or group of languages would be spoken over a rather large area. This criteria is not fulfilled in any other part of Africa with the exception of the Western Sudan, and in particular is focused on the Mandingos and their location on the upper Niger. The Mandingos exhibit Negro agriculture at its fullest, spreading in all directions at the expense of their more backward neighbors, they have spread west, south, and east, cutting across other groups and even north into some of the oases of the Sahara. The Niger and its environs must await the precision of radio-carbon dating. From these inferences it can be concluded that the Mandingo people, situated around the headwaters of the Niger less than a 1,000 miles from the Atlantic Ocean, were the inventors of agriculture in Negro Africa. It is no accident, then, nor can it be a surprise, that these civilizations that we have been describing could grow in this area. The clues, and their piecing together with the aid of archeological research, will mark with precision what can only be a very strong inference drawn from the facts; ethnographic and agricultural distribution are important criteria along with the discovery of metal working in assessing evidence historically. "We cannot ignore (says Professor Murdock) the vulgar assumption, widespread among Asiatics as well as Europeans, that the Negro is an inferior race incapable of making any substantial contribution to civilization, with its corollary that all complex manifestations of culture in Africa south of the Sahara must have emanated from some other and 'higher' race like the Caucasoid 'Hamites.'"

The history of the Berber peoples is much more than the raiding and pillaging of Timbuktu, and their role in the caravan traffic, they are a specific and fascinating society in themselves. It is true that warfare has characterized the life of the Berber as far back as we can go, which is to the Arab invasions of the seventh and eleventh century, when they occupied the whole of the western and central Sahara. Where the Berbers have resisted the Arabizing influence, and the cultural penetration that resulted from their fragmentation in the eleventh century by the Arab invasion, they have rejected the caste system of the Arabs. The Tuaregs are the only group among the Berbers who have let this caste system permeate their society. The Berbers are sometimes called by the Arabs "the Christians of the desert." It is highly unlikely that they ever professed Christianity, but they could be safely said to have been influenced by it.

The Berbers, without the Arabic influence, were remarkably egalitarian. Although they had a class system, there was no serfdom and rarely slavery. The government, or the community at large, was managed by an assembly, the assembly appointed executive agents, the larger area was broken down into district councils. When a district was at war, and there always had been much blood feuding, the council appointed a military leader with absolute authority for the duration of the emergency. The Berbers had a very complicated system which could only be referred to as a "balance of power" between the numerous sub-divisions of the larger group (there are 29 groups who still speak Berber, {G. P. Murdock}, as distinct from those who speak Arabic). Those that speak Berber, generally still retain their ancient customs, although there has been much diffusion of Arabic culture, it is in the mountain areas that the purity is maintained. Though this "balance of power" rarely prevented war, it had a peace-enforcing mechanism. The 3,000 years of recorded history that we have at our disposal tell us that the Berbers infinitely preferred their way of careful balance, even with its breakdowns into bloody warfare, to any kind of despotic or authoritarian rule.

The Tuaregs, called camel nomads, despise agriculture and are Arabized Berbers. They have abandoned their ancestral way of life, originated from Tripolitania (Libya). The Arabs gave them the name of the "Muleththemin," meaning the veiled people. The men up to this day wear veils with only their eyes exposed, it is they that use the cross symbol so prominately as a decoration. They were not only migratory but predatory, and extorted tribute from the caravan traffic; on the positive side they also helped make the Sahara a passable highway by keeping the oases cared for. It was their ancestors, who first initiated the trans-Saharan trade, thought to have begun as early as the third millenium B.C.

The Tuareg departs from its related tribes by the existence of a domestic caste system, which is said to have been totally adopted from the Arabs. Although much eroded by time, this system still unhappily exists today in the now small town of Timbuktu. It is frowned upon by the present day government, which, together with the world community, is seeking its eradication. The caste system is of interest for the reason that through it the history of the Western Sudan can be traced, and then seen from a different perspective. First there are religious nobles or Marabouts. Following from there, there are five separate castes: 1. the Imochar, the ruler who produces nothing, who conducts warfare and completely dominates the community; 2. the Imrad, who is a vassal, bears arms for the leader and pays tribute to him; 3. the Bella or Haratin, Negro slaves who farm and pay taxes; 4. the Iklan, privately owned slaves gained through capture or purchased for domestic service; 5. the Inaden, Negro smiths, leatherworkers, and other artisans who are considered to be outcasts. This elucidation shows the daily design of society as it was lived in a very important city of the area.

An important detour must be made in order to comment on what some detractors of the African have called "their tradition of slavery." The tradition of African slavery, aside from the Tuareg which is particular to their culture, is a far different institution from that developed by the Europeans. The African variety is usually referred to as being a benign or domestic institution. Black African slaves were in the main war captives and naturally given a humble status by their captor. Some groups banished undesirable persons by performing a ritual breaking of their kinship, and thereby generally speaking they could be "sold into slavery," in other words they were removed from their kinsmen. This was household slavery. Some slaves attained a high status in the households to which they were attached, and it was not uncommon for an African to take up arms in behalf of his insulted "slave."

European slavery was primarily economic. The domestic slave of Africa was a far cry from the "bond servant" of medieval Europe. A person was sold into bondage in order to pay off a debt. The idea of the "bond servant" was completely tied to the "ethic" of feudalism.

When the two types of slavery met, most likely in the markets of Africa, Africans were not opposed to selling slaves, as they understood them, and Europeans were hardly averse for moral reasons, then, to buy them. At first many of the Negroes were sold on a contractual basis, for a limited period. At no time did the African visualize that the man sold was to become a permanent part in building the new economies that emerged from their soulless and backbreaking labor.

Returning now to the peoples of the Western Sudan, we come to the Hausas, who now make their home in the Nigerian Plateau region in Northern Nigeria. The country eastwards from the Niger to Lake Chad is referred to as Hausa. Various peoples live in what used to be known as the Seven Hausa States. There are some non-Moslems among them. They are an ancient people, with much experience in Saharan trade, and have developed a considerable amount of cultural unity, much like the nations of Europe. Their literature is considerable, among it is the famous "Kano Chronicle." The Chronicle written in Arabic in the latter part of the 1800's catalogues the battles of the Middle Ages. The Hausa were conquered by the Fulani in the 19th century.

The Fulani, wherever they are, are in contrast to their neighbors in both physique and culture. The ancestral Fulani, it is thought, come from the middle region of the Senegal Valley and the savanna region of Fouta Toro. They arrived in Hausa in about the 13th century. Many have intermarried with the Negroes and their infiltration was peaceful and disturbed no one. The town Fulani (Fulanin Gidda) are Moslems, while the pastoralists (Borooje or Cow Fulani) were pagans. The town Fulani, a highly intelligent people, became a kind of aristocracy, looking down on the pastoral nomads. Both were welcome wherever they went. The Cow Fulani were valued for their agicultural skills. They mingled with the Mandingos in the 12th and 13th century, and in the 14th penetrated eastward to the Soninke. In the 16th century they went from Senegal to Guinea. A considerable number settled in Gobir (a Hausa state in the Northern Region of Nigeria). Usman don Fodio, the national hero of the Fulani of Hausa was born in Gobir. The history of this man's career, lit by the fires of his Islamic faith is a book in itself. Suffice it to say, this ruler of the faithful embarked on a holy war in 1804 and 1809 and successively conquered the Hausa states, and established a Fulani emir in each territory. At the time of his death he divided his dominions between his son and his brother. They ruled most of Northern Nigeria until the British colonized the area.

The Songhai have been adequately covered in the chapter on their Empire. The SuSu or SoSo people are part of the larger Mandingo family and are Moslems. The Mossi are a mercantile people, they live in the region of the interior watershed of the Volta River. Islam has had little effect on them.

As the great West African territorial empires were collapsing, and their influence subsiding, the African peoples were simultaneously experiencing the intrusion of the European. With them came the blight and trauma of the continent, European style slavery. Christianity too entered, impelled as it was to extend its morality outward, along with the colonial administration. The slave trade had one more cultural dimension, its American dimension. The Negroes had to undergo the defiling experience of not only being herded like cattle to the New World, but, when having arrived to find that not only was their culture rejected, but that they were rejected by American culture.

It was only when the economies of Europe were sufficiently developed with the help of cheap black labor, that the "savage" became "noble." A small and magnificant minority of deeply religious Christians, fired by humanitarian ideals, articulated the guilt of centuries for millions so effectively, that slavery began to diminish in the 18th century, but it was not abolished until the 19th century.

Up until 1884 the European foothold in West Africa was merely a toehold on the rim of the West Coast in the form of trading stations. Europeans rarely ventured into the interior. In the latter part of the 18th century, explorers found impetus through societies formed for the exploration of the African interior. It was with this encouragement that Mungo Park solved the riddle of the source of the Niger, and a century later the Sahara was crossed and Lake Chad was discovered.

The course of the Niger was charted by Clapperton and the Landers. René Caillié, a Frenchman, visited Timbuktu in 1828. Heinrich Barth, a German geographer, made his trip to Africa in the 19th century, and brought back with him important ethnological studies. By 1914 colonization was complete. The scramble for Africa was officially over, at least for the Europeans, but the full impact of the colonial administration was yet to be experienced.

Colonialism, as many people are fond of saying, "brought order to Africa." What it actually did was to freeze the movements of a dynamic people, who were constantly on the move. Whether the bureaucratic zeal of the colonial administrator for putting things into "order" actually helped to further crystallize the cultures of these once mobile societies, now held in check by "legalized" boundaries, is difficult to prove. Many Africans found, for various reasons, that the enforced "territorial paralysis" of colonialism amounted to a deprivation. Containing movement and drawing borders, it disrupted the traditional centers of power to such an extent, that it could hardly be called a condition of "peace and stability," that merited the admiration of Europeans in the thros of their own domestic wars at the time. Africans were destined to do without the "checks and balances" that operate from open conflict with each other. The African continent, acknowledged by most authorities to have been in chaos both in the west and east due to the slave trade, could hardly have been called an "ordered" society. Little real internal order could have existed following the abandonment of the slave trade, which was followed by the imposition of police methods by the colonial administration to keep things "quiet." So much of the "colonial story" has been told, and splendidly, with more than a few traces of heroism, so dear to those like that driven man, David Livingston. Livingston characterized Africa as the "dark continent"; there is little doubt that the African felt that way about Europe!

The past longing for independence culminated in the 1960's, and brought forth a multitude of states, who were granted admission to the United Nations. They brought with them diversity, iconoclasm, and many truths. The United Nation's debates in the 1960's found many delegates shaking their earphones (used for the translation purposes) with surprise, as the Africans retold the story of their European "tutors" with a very different twist and without the accustomed "and so they lived happily ever after." The reaction of the former colonial powers (the United States' reaction was similar) to this ran from puzzlement, to a kind of patronizing understanding, right through to one of distress, and then in some cases plain distaste. The African entrance, en masse to the United Nations, proved to be very disturbing, and upset the equilibrium of the Western powers.

The plain fact was, that Africa had never been asleep, it was not just awakening in that fond journalistic phrase, but it had been constantly in a state of movement and development, like other peoples of the world, and that, the appearance in the United Nations of numbers of new nation-states in the 20th century sense, was not looked upon by them as a gift that they must be grateful to the colonial powers for. They had survived man's brutality to man, the slave trade, without being destroyed, both physically and spiritually as others had *not* done, and they had adapted to the colonial system in such a way that the changes that it did effect could not serve as sustenance for the African soul.

Colonialism has been described as a "working mis-understanding" with an "absentee sovereign." In the colonial situation, both Africa and Europe viewed society in terms of their own cultures, at times these cultures converged, but there never was any real communication. There was much fear, suspicion, sometimes tyranny and a great deal of stupidity. The absentee landlord or sovereign always made decisions on the basis of values or conditions that existed at home, and hardly thought of the colony in terms of its own uniqueness. What it amounted to, was different responses stemming from two different outlooks.

Through what is called interpenetration of cultures, changes began to take place in the African, and in their societies. Up until the time that a man is a "tribal person", he is by no stretch of the imagination a deprived person, he has status, opportunity, a place in the group and experiences his culture to the fullest extent possible. It is when limits are imposed upon people that they become restless and frustrated. The colonial powers by educating Africans, and then stopping the training at a low level brought the frustrations of those who could not see why they should be deprived from advancing, to the point of explosion. It was then that they become "deprived" in the usual sense of the word. From that moment they begin adapting themselves again, for the sake of survival, in order to escape this trap which was felt to be a tyranny.

Along with their efforts to rewin the political kingdom, they too, have felt the call to reestablish an African presence, which went beyond statecraft to a search for selfhood. This was enunciated as early as 1956, in Paris, when The Society of African Culture called its First Conference of Negro Writers and Artists and defined its task in part as, seeking "an emergence of an African personality from the accretion of Western culture, which colonization has thrown into disequilibrium and servitude." Along with the concept of the "African personality," which seems to bear a close relation to the African's position on the international stage, there is the idea of "negritude." All these visions of the self seek to be recognized as universal values, rather than indicating the racial narrowness that has sometimes been attributed to them.

Bibliography

Africanus, L.   The History and Description of Africa.
                   3 Vols. Hakluyt Society. London. 1896.

Bovill, E. W.   Caravans of the Old Sahara. London.
                   1933.

Bovill, E. W.   The Golden Trade of the Moors. Lon-
                   don. 1958.

Bohanan, P.   Africa and Africans. New York. 1964.

Briggs, L. C.   Tribes of the Sahara. Harvard Univer-
                   sity Press. Cambridge. 1960.

Brown, L.   Africa, a Natural History. Random
                   House. 1965.

Bunbury, E. H.   History of Ancient Geography. 2 Vols.
                   1879.

Davidson, B.   The African Past. Boston. 1961.

Delafosse, M.   The Negroes of Africa. Washington, D.C.
                   1930.

Delafosse, M.   Haut-Senegal-Niger. Paris. 1912.

Dubois, W. E. B.   The World and Africa. New York. 1947.

Fage, J. D.   An Atlas of African History. London.
                   1958.

Fage, J. D.   An Introduction to the History of West
                     Africa. Cambridge. London. 1955.

Flint, J. E.   Nigeria and Ghana. New York.

Gailey, H. A.   A History of the Gambia. Praeger. New
                     York. 1965.

Hallett, Robin.   The Penetration of Africa. Praeger. New
                     York. 1965.

Healy and   The Map Approach to African History.
Verne-Hodge.   London. 1962.

Herskovits, M. J.   The Myth of the Negro Past.

Herskovits, M. J.   The Human Factor in Changing Africa.
                     Knopf. New York. 1962.

Herskovits, M. J.   Dahomey. 2 Vols. New York 1935.

Labouret, H.   Africa before the White Man. New York.

Latham, N.   A Sketchmap History of West Africa.

Leuzinger, E.   The Art of Africa. Crown. New York.
                     1960.

Miner, H.   The Primitive City of Timbuktu. Anchor.
                     New York. 1965.

Murdock, G.   Africa, its Peoples and their Culture
                     History. McGraw-Hill. New York. 1959.

Parrinder, E. G.   West African Religion. London. 1949.

Rouch, Jean   Les Songhay. Presses Universitaires de
                     France. 1954.

Tooley, R. V.   Maps and Mapmakers. 2nd edition. 1952.

Ward, W. E. F.   A History of Ghana. London. 1958.

| Westermann, Diedrich | Geschichte Afrikas. Staatenbildungen Sudlich Der Sahara. Greven-Verlag. Koln. 1952. |

Other Sources

African Studies Bulletin. Columbia University. Vol. V. No. 4. December 1962. Report of the Fifth Annual Meeting of the African Studies Association. A paper by Dr. D. McCall of Boston University. "Trans-Saharan Interaction: Its significance in African History."

African Studies Bulletin. Columbia University. Vol. VI. No. 4. Raymond A. Mauny of University of California. Report of the Sixth Annual meeting of the African Studies Association. "The Influence of the Gold Trade on Medieval Africa's Economy."

Journal of African History. Volume IV. 1963. No. 3. "The Kings of Mali."

Glossary

ABU BAKR—After the death of Ibn Yacin, who was killed in battle about 1057, control passed into the hands of Abu Bakr, whose headquarters was near Marrakech (Morocco). Under his leadership the Almoravids conquered the Ghana Empire.

AFRICANUS, LEO—A Moor, born in Granada. He was educated in Fez (Morocco) and made his memorable trip to West Africa before he was 20 years old. From the copious notes that he took there emerged *The History and Description of Africa.*

ALMORAVIDS—Were a confederation of Saharan Berber tribes. They ruled north-western Africa and Moslem Spain in the 11th and 12th century.

ANTHROPOLOGY—The study of human culture. Human behavior as conditioned by social organization.

ARCHEOLOGY—Is concerned with the material remains of man's past. It consists of two aspects: the discovery and reclamation of ancient remains, from which analysis and interpretation is made.

AUDOGHAST—Once a Berber town located in Mauritania. A great market center.

BAKHOY—A river in Mali. It is thought that the Mandingo kingdom of Mali originated from the upper Bakhoy eastwards across the Niger River, its capital was Jeriba, where extensive ruins have been found.

BARBARY—A belt of country separating the Mediterranean from the Sahara Desert; it extends from Tripoli in the east to the Atlantic Ocean in the west.

BERBER—The only present day criterion for delineating this group is their language. They are too varied a people to constitute a single and distinct entity. The name commonly designated the population from the Egyptian frontier to the shores of the Atlantic and the great bend of the Niger.

BORNU—A small ancient state, west of Lack Chad, which reached its height in the 16th century. Their history can be traced back about 1,000 years.

BORGU—Was a small country in what is now northern Nigeria.

CAILLE, RENE—A Frenchman, who in the early 18th century, disguised himself as an Arab and made his way to Jenne, and from there travelled down the Niger and reached Timbuktu, which by then had declined from the heights described by Leo Africanus.

CYRENAICA—The eastern, and territorially the largest province of modern day Libya. In ancient times it was founded by the Greeks, who made it a great intellectual center of the classical world. It prospered for two centuries, and its subsequent history is one of steady decline due to the increasing insecurity of the desert frontiers. The northern half of the ancient district of Cyrenaica was known as Pentapolis from its possession of five considerable cities.

DANAKIL—A people who resided in what is now the state of Somalia.

DENDI—The traditional home of the Songhai people, located not far above the Busa rapids in what is now northern Nigeria.

EL GHABA—One of two towns that made up the capital of the Ghana Empire, it was the pagan quarter.

ES-SADI—An historian who lived and wrote in Timbuktu.

FULANI—A pastoral people who have been thought to have been the "alien" element that swept into Tekrur, and lower Senegal. These "alien people" intermarried with the people of that region and produced the Fulani, they spread eastward throughout the Sudan and into the Cameroons.

GAO—Became the capital of the great Songhai Empire. Gao was divided into two quarters, one Moslem, the other pagan, also an important commercial center.

HADJ—The name given to the pilgrimage that devout Moslems made to the holy city of Mecca.

HAUSA—A Negro people found chiefly in northern Nigeria, and in what was called French West Africa. They share a common language, similar customs and origin. They never formed an empire, but were subjects of many different kingdoms. Islam was introduced to them in the latter part of the 14th century.

HEJIRA—Mohammads flight from Mecca in A.D. 622, later taken as the first year of the Moslem era.

HERODOTUS—The historian of the ancient world, whose works preceeded that of Ptolemy.

IBN BATTUTA—An Arab traveler born in Tangier. His last long journey took him to Timbuktu and Mali. He dictated the account of his travels to a scholar.

IBN HAUKAL—A contemporary of Masudi, also born in Baghdad, is consdiered to be the first explorer of West Africa, and it is from him that we have the earliest account of the Western Sudan. In his 25 years of travel, which he collected into a volume called *Book of Ways and Provinces,* he claimed to have included in this geography everything of interest "to either princes or peoples."

IBN KHALDUN—From the biographical notes in the *Encyclopedia of Islam* we see that his statesmanlike ability led him to hold many important administrative offices. He played an important and sometimes perilous role in the politics of North Africa and Spain. His book the *History of the Berbers* was the fruit of 50 years of work. He had studied with care, books and chronicles, as well as diplomatic and official documents. His Mukaddima (written in the 2nd half of the 14th century) or preface was described as the most important work of the age.

JENNE—According to tradition, withstood 99 assaults of the Mali kings. Founded in the 13th century by the Soninke, it is located in the fertile river and lake region, not far from the banks of the Niger. An important market center for the gold-salt trade; also flourished as a cultural center.

JUDAR—A Spainard from Granada, led the first Moroccan invasion across the desert in order to attack the ancient Songhai Empire.

JERIBA—Capital of the small, ancient kingdom of Mali which was located on the upper Bakhoy River, situated in modern day Mali. Its history before the 13th century is a blind spot, what is known, is that one of its rulers, called Baramendana became a convert to Islam in the early days of the Almoravid movement.

KANGABA—Thought to be a possible site of the ancient capital of the Mali Empire, it is just a short distance downstream on the Niger, below Mali's present day capital of Bamako.

KEBBI—A vassal state of the Songhai king, Askia.

MAGHCHAREN—Another name for the Tuareg, used by Es-Sadi.

MAGHREB (or MAGHRIB)—Name given by Arab writers to that part of Africa which modern writers on geography call Barbary, or Africa Minor, which includes Tripolitania, Tunisia, Algeria, Morocco. The name means the west, the setting sun.

MANSA MUSA—Grandson of Sundiata, most splendid and accomplished of all the Mandingo Emperors.

MASUDI—An Arab from Baghdad, whose travels took him to such places as China and Madagascar. He is the first to note the unusual way in which the gold trade of the early Ghana Empire was conducted.

MEDICI, POPE LEO X—Son of Lorenzo the Magnificent, who was a patron of the arts. This Pope gave Leo Africanus the name of Giovanni Leone.

MORION—A foot soldiers visorless high-crested helmet, of Spanish origin, with the edge turned up.

MOSSI—A people inhabitating roughly the area of what is now the state of Upper Volta. These people had their own political system which lasted for 800 years. They warred with the peoples to the north of them, but were never conquered themselves.

MULAY AHMED EL-MANSUR—Sultan of Morocco in 1578.

NIANI—Capital of the old Mali Empire, is said to have been located between the modern states of Guinea and Mali.

NIGER RIVER—Largest river in West Africa, the 10th largest river in the world. It is 2,600 miles long and rises in the hills of the Futa Jallon (Guinea).

PARK, MUNGO—A British explorer of the Niger River, who endured many privations in his quest. He reached it in July, 1796. Worn down by sickness he had to stay in the area for 7 months, while being nursed back to health by an African trader. In England he was thought dead, when he made a sensational return three and a half years later. He was killed on a later journey on the Niger by some Africans.

PTOLMEY (CLAUDIUS PTOLMEY)—The great geographer of the 2nd century A.D. who lived in Alexandria. His geography is a gazeteer, in which he lists large numbers of rivers and mountains along with towns and tribes.

RADIOCARBON DATING—Application of one of the newest scientific tools (measurement of radio activity) to archeology. It involves measuring the ratio of radioactive carbon (c 14) to regular carbon (c 12) in a given specimen. This ratio bears a mathematical relationship to the age of the object under analysis.

SAHARA—World's largest desert. Stretches across Africa from the Atlantic coast through Egypt to the Red Sea, beyond which the desert continues into Arabia and Iran. Its greatest west-east extension exceeds 3,000 miles. The Ahaggar and Tibesti mountains are in what is called the Saharan plateau.

SIJILMASA—A town founded in the 8th century. It is thought to have been located in lower Morocco. It was a place through which caravans came and went. The earliest reference to it was by Ibn Haukal in the 10th century. Its importance to the gold trade allowed it to flourish long after the collapse of the Ghana Empire.

SONGHAI—The name of a people and also of the most powerful Empire of the Western Sudan.

SORKO—The Songhai were divided into two hostile clans, one was the Sorko who were fisherman and the other were called Gabibi, who were farmers. The Sorko being more mobile, dominated the Gabibi.

SUNDIATA—A great Mandino chief.

SU SU (SO SO)—A kingdom made up of the Su or So people, which was at one time part of the Ghana Empire.

SURAME—The name of the Seven Walls at which Askia was defeated by the Kebbi.

TABORET—A small drum with one head, like a tambourine with jungles. Used as an accompaniment to a pipe or fife, both being played by the same person.

TADMEKKA—An important desert market.

TAODENI—Salt mines that were located in the north of present day Mali.

TARIKH-es-SOUDAN—A collection of papers by the Timbuktu born scholar Es-Sadi, who apparently drew upon works and chronicles that have not been passed down to us. The Tarikh was discovered by Heinrich Barth, a German explorer, in 1853 at Gwandu in northern Nigeria.

TAKEDDA—East of Gao, located in the desert. A coppermining town.

TEKRUR—A small kingdom, whose inhabitants converted to Islam in about the 11th century. It was located approximately in the vicinity of Senegal.

TILUNTANE—A Berber chief of the Lemtuna tribe, whose headquarters were located in Mauritania.

TONDIBI—A town 35 miles from Gao. The Songhai troops were badly beaten by the Moroccans there.

TRIPOLITANIA—Located in Libya, the home of semi-nomadic tribes.

TUAREG—A nomadic people who once occupied the whole of the central and western Sahara. They are tall, slim and generally fair-skinned. They are a branch of the Berber peoples. The Tuareg as skilled caravan drivers controlled many of the important caravan routes that linked North Africa with the lands south of the Sahara. Their history goes back to the Arab invasions of the 7th and 11th century.

TAGHAZA—Located deep in the desert. The salt of the Taghaza mines was traded for gold, so short was the supply of this mineral south of the Sahara.

WANGARA—The general name of a place, and a people. They mined most of the West African gold, and they managed to keep the exact location a secret. They did this by using the method called "silent trade" or barter. The fields are thought to be in the Bambuk-Bure vicinity. Wangara was thought to have been another name for the Soninke people.

WESTERN SUDAN—It is the term used by historians for the general area approximately from the Red Sea to the Atlantic Ocean; including the land which is west of Lake Chad.

Index

El-Mansur, Mulay Ahmet (Sultan of Morocco), 56-58, 80.
El-Omari, 9, 24, 25, 29.
El-Ufrani, 56.
Encyclopedia of Islam, 79.
Es-Sadi, 8, 47, 55-56, 59, 78.
Es-Saheli, 30, 40.
Ethiopia, 27, 63.

Fagbine lake, 49.
Faleme, 17.
Fertile Crescent, 63.
Fez, 40, 41.
Fouta Toro, 68.
Fulani, 48-49, 67-68, 78.

Gabibi, 81.
Gambia, 8, 23-24.
Gao, 30, 34, 41, 45-46, 48, 50-53, 56-57, 78, 82.
Ghana, 3-5, 23-26, 39, 41, 62.
    Empire of, 7-20, 78, 80-81.
Gobir, 53, 68.
Gold Coast, 7.
Gonja dynasty, 3.
Granada, 30, 40, 57, 77, 79.
Guinea, 8, 10, 24, 49, 68, 80.

Hadj, 24, 50, 52, 78.
Haratin, 66.
Hausa, 23, 53-56, 67-68, 78.
Hejira, 8, 79.
Henry the Navigator, Prince, 49.
Herodotus, 17, 79.
Hershkovits, Melville, 62.
The History and Description of Africa, 33, 77.
History of the Berbers, 41, 79.
Human Factor in Changing Africa, 62.

Ibadan, 2.
Ibadan University workshop, 1965, 2.
Ibn Battuta, 9, 17, 24-25, 37-40, 79.
Ibn Haukal, 9-10, 79, 81.
Ibn Khaldun, 9, 14, 19, 24, 33, 40-42, 79.
Ibn Yacin, 12, 18, 77.
Ife heads, 4.
Iklan, 66.
Imrad, 66.
Inaden, 66.
India, 39, 63.

Iraqui, 63.
Islam, 3, 5, 12-13, 18-19, 23-24, 26, 37, 48, 50-51, 62-63, 68, 79.

Jedala, 12.
Jenne, 25, 47-48, 51, 58-59, 61, 78-79.
Jeriba, 26, 77, 79.
Juba, 61.
Judar, 57,´79.
Jewish persecution in Africa, 50-51.

Kamba, 40.
Kanem, 41.
Kangaba, 26, 80.
Kano, 23, 51, 53.
Kano Chronicle, 67.
Kanta, King of Kebbi, 54-55.
Katsina, 23, 51, 53, 55.
Kebbi (the Kebbawa), 54-55, 80-81.
Kente cloth, 7.
Koran, 31, 35, 39.
Kukia, 45.
Kumbi (Saleh), 8, 13, 14, 16.

Landers, Richard Lemon, 69.
Las Cuevas. *See* Judar.
Lemtuna tribes, 11-12.
Leo Africanus. *See* Africanus, Leo.
Leptis Magna, 61.
L'Islam Noir, 4.
Livingston, David, 70.

Madagascar, 9.
Maghan, 33-34.
Maghreb, 56, 80.
Mahmud Pasha ben-Zegun, 57-59.
Mali, 5, 18, 20, 45-46, 49, 52, 53, 56, 77, 79-80, 82.
    Empire of, 23-42, 80.
    Federation of, 23.
Mami ben-Barun, 58.
Mandingos, 23, 27, 40, 45-46, 48-49, 56, 64, 68, 80-81.
Mani-Koura, 26.
Mansa Ule, 27.
Mansa Musa, 27-31, 33-34, 39, 45, 52, 80.
Mansa Sulayman, 33-34, 39-40.
Marabouts, 66.